Volume 22

By
Natsuki Takaya

HAMBURG // LONDON // LOS ANGELES // TOKYO

Fruits Basket

Table of Contents

Chapter 126 11
Chapter 127 41
Chapter 128 72
Chapter 129 105
Chapter 130 135
Chapter 131 167
Fans Basket 198

STORY SO FAR...

Hello, I'm Tohru Honda, and I have come to know a terrible secret. After the death of my mother, I was living by myself in a tent, when the Sohma family took me in. I soon learned that the Sohma family lives with a curse! Each family member is possessed by the vengeful spirit of an animal from the Chinese Zodiac. Whenever one of them becomes weak or is hugged by a member of the opposite sex, that person changes into his or her Zodiac animal!

...SOME SORT OF TRIGGER THAT WILL BREAK HIS CURSE!

...I'M GOING TO HAVE TO CREATE...

IF I WANT TO SAVE KYO...

Tohru Honda

The ever-optimistic heroine of our story. An orphan, she now lives in Shigure's house, along with Yuki and Kyo, and is the only person outside of the family who knows the Sohma family's curse.

Yuki Sohma, the Rat

Soft-spoken. Self-esteem issues. At school, he's called "Prince Yuki."

Kyo Sohma, the Cat

The Cat who was left out of the Zodiac. Hates Yuki, leeks and miso. But mostly Yuki.

Kagura Sohma, the Boar

Bashful, yet headstrong. Determined to marry Kyo, even if it kills him.

Fruits Basket
Volume 22

Natsuki Takaya

Fruits Basket Volume 22
Created by Natsuki Takaya

Translation - Alethea & Athena Nibley
English Adaptation - Lianne Sentar
Copy Editor - Stephanie Duchin
Retouch and Lettering - Star Print Brokers
Production Artist - Michael Paolilli
Graphic Designer - Tina Corrales

Editor - Alexis Kirsch
Pre-Production Supervisor - Vicente Rivera, Jr.
Print-Production Specialist - Lucas Rivera
Managing Editor - Vy Nguyen
Senior Designer - Louis Csontos
Senior Designer - James Lee
Senior Editor - Bryce P. Coleman
Senior Editor - Jenna Winterberg
Associate Publisher - Marco F. Pavia
President and C.O.O. - John Parker
C.E.O. and Chief Creative Officer - Stu Levy

A  Manga

TOKYOPOP and are trademarks or registered trademarks of TOKYOPOP Inc.

TOKYOPOP Inc.
5900 Wilshire Blvd. Suite 2000
Los Angeles, CA 90036

E-mail: info@TOKYOPOP.com
Come visit us online at www.TOKYOPOP.com

FRUITS BASKET by Natsuki Takaya
© 2007 Natsuki Takaya
All rights reserved.
First published in Japan in 2007 by HAKUSENSHA, INC., Tokyo
English language translation rights in the United States of
America, Canada and the United Kingdom arranged with
HAKUSENSHA, INC., Tokyo through Tuttle-Mori Agency Inc.,
Tokyo English text copyright © 2009 TOKYOPOP Inc.

All rights reserved. No portion of this book may be reproduced or transmitted in any form or by any means without written permission from the copyright holders. This manga is a work of fiction. Any resemblance to actual events or locales or persons, living or dead, is entirely coincidental.

ISBN: 978-1-4278-0683-3

First TOKYOPOP printing: March 2009
10 9 8 7 6 5 4 3 2 1
Printed in the USA

Fruits Basket Characters

Mabudachi Trio

Shigure Sohma, the Dog
Enigmatic, mischievous and a little perverted. A popular novelist.

Hatori Sohma, the Dragon
Family doctor to the Sohmas. Only thing he can't cure is his broken heart.

Ayame Sohma, the Snake
Yuki's older brother. A proud and playful drama queen…er, king. Runs a costume shop.

Saki Hanajima
"Hana-chan." Can sense people's "waves." Goth demeanor scares her classmates.

Arisa Uotani
"Uo-chan." A tough-talking "Yankee" who looks out for her friends.

Tohru's Best Friends

Hiro Sohma, the Ram (or sheep)

This caustic tyke is skilled at throwing verbal barbs, but he has a soft spot for Kisa.

Momiji Sohma, the Rabbit

Half German. He's older than he looks. His mother rejected him because of the Sohma curse. His little sister, Momo, has been kept from him most of her life.

Hatsuharu Sohma, the Ox

The nicest of guys, except when he goes "Black." Then you'd better watch out. He was once in a relationship with Rin.

Kisa Sohma, the Tiger

Kisa became shy and self-conscious due to constant teasing by her classmates. Yuki, who has similar insecurities, feels particularly close to Kisa.

Fruits Basket Characters

Isuzu "Rin" Sohma, the Horse

She was once in a relationship with Hatsuharu (Haru)...and Tohru leaves her rather cold. Rin is full of pride, and she can't stand the amount of deference the other Sohma family members give Akito.

Ritsu Sohma, the Monkey

This shy, kimono-wearing member of the Sohma family is gorgeous. But this "she" is really a he!! Cross-dressing calms his nerves.

Kureno Sohma, the Rooster (or bird)

He is Akito's very favorite, and spends almost all of his time on the Sohma estate, tending to Akito's every desire. Kureno was born possessed by the spirit of the Bird, but his curse broke long ago...which means we've never seen him transformed. He pities Akito's loneliness, and can't bring himself to leave her.

"God"

Akito Sohma

The head of the Sohma clan. A dark figure of many secrets. Treated with fear and reverence. It has recently been revealed that Akito is actually a woman!

...!
WHAT?! OF--
course
not
BLEEEEEGGGHHH!
WHAT WAS THAT?!
YIKES!
Cough
Cough cough
What's wrong with you?!
YOU'RE PUKING IN A PUBLIC PLACE!
Cough
... THE THREAD OF MY NERVES ...
...JUST SNAP-PED.
THAT DOESN'T MAKE ANY SENSE! AND CRIPES, YOU'RE DISGUSTING!
Censored for the sake of the audience.

I FEEL A LITTLE BETTER...

WHO WOULDN'T, AFTER EMPTYING THE TANK?!

UM...

UM... ONII-CHAN.

HERE.

LOOK, YOU.

Agh.

...THANKS.

FORGET ABOUT THANKING HER AND JUST CLEAN UP, OKAY?

I'LL HELP YOU.

FORGET IT--I CAN DO IT MYSELF.

I SAID I'M HELPING!

I WANNA SEE YOU.

Let's borrow some cleaning supplies.

Yeah.

......

IF I'M HALLUCINATING ABOUT HER NOW...

...I MUST HAVE IT BAD.

I REALLY WANNA SEE YOU.

Chapter 127

I'D HEARD BITS OF THE STORY FROM TOHRU.

AND I MET WITH AKITO SOHMA...

...JUST THE OTHER DAY.

WELL.

TOHRU-KUN DOESN'T THINK OF IT...

...AS ANYONE'S FAULT.

AND...

I HEARD.

ABOUT KURENO.

I DON'T KNOW WHAT SHE'S TOLD YOU.

BUT HER INJURIES.

THEY'RE...

...MY FAULT.

...TO WORRY ABOUT ME.

SERIOUSLY?

SHE SHOULDN'T HAVE TIME...

Diiiing dooong

Daang doong

YIKES! THAT SCARED ME.

...WHAT THE HELL IS WRONG WITH HIM?

WELL, HE MARCHED IN HERE AND SAID HE WAS GONNA SEE TOHRU.

Like an upstanding young man.

SO WE TOLD HIM THE TRUTH-- AND LOOK AT HIM NOW.

...W-WAIT.

..........!

"WE DON'T THINK TOHRU-KUN WANTS TO SEE YOU RIGHT NOW."

THAT TRUTH.

BECAUSE THAT'S LOW, EVEN FOR--

WAIT, WAIT, WAIT

MESSING WITH YOU?

ARE YOU MESSING WITH ME?

YOU DON'T UNDERSTAND A THING.

DO YOU, LITTLE BOY?

DO YOU THINK W[E] WOULD LIE ABO[UT] TOHRU-KUN'S FEELINGS

WOULD I...?

...JUST TO TEASE YOU?

STILL....

I KNOW WHAT YOU'RE TALKING ABOUT.
WHENEVER HIS NAME CAME UP, HONDA-SAN WAS OBVIOUSLY SCARED.
CLAAAAANG
...
IT'S LIKE... SHE DOESN'T WANT TO SEE HIM.
CLAAAAAAANG
OR MAYBE ...
Yeah, you're right!
TOHRU-KUN SEEMS TO THINK HE DUMPED HER.
INDEED.
S...
Scared?!
NICE WORK, GENIUS.

Fruits Basket

Nice to meet you and hello. I'm Takaya, presenting Volume 22. The cover has Tohru's Daddy on it this time around. I was going to make the color behind him white, but then he would end up looking like Akkii, so I changed it.

(It might not matter much, but in my head, Akkii has a white image.)

Now then. In the magazine, Furuba has safely reached its final chapter. The next volume will be the last graphic novel.

Sometimes people ask me if that makes me sad, but it doesn't-- not really, anyway. An author never **actually** says goodbye to her works.

It's true that a manga ends, but it's something that will continue to exist inside me forever. Maybe I'm not explaining it very well? Basically, what I want to say is that I think the ones who will really be sad will be the people who have kept reading and loving Furuba.

Thank you very much. Now please enjoy Furuba Volume 22!

Let's go.

I'm going home.

WELL, WHEN SOMEONE TELLS YOU THEY'RE DISILLU- SIONED...

IT'S EASY TO INTERPRET THAT...

...AS THEM SAYING "GET LOST."

WHY DOES SHE THINK THAT?!

WHY THE HELL DIDN'T YOU GUYS TELL ME SOMETHING THAT IMPORTANT?!

TH-THAT'S THE WORST KIND OF MISUNDER- STANDING!

Um...

You think so?

Is it?

EVERYBODY KNOWS HOW YOU TWO FEEL ABOUT EACH OTHER. THAT DOESN'T BOTHER YOU?

A-AND IF I DON'T SEE HER SOON, IT'LL BE LIKE I'M CONFIRMING IT!

NO ONE CARES ABOUT WHAT'S CONVENIENT FOR YOU, STUPID.
IT DOESN'T CHANGE THE FACT THAT YOU MADE HER CRY. YOU PISS ME OFF. YOU'D BETTER DO SOME SERIOUS REFLECTION, DUMBASS!
Baldy!
Wha?!
SO SHE IS JUST GETTING BACK AT ME.
ANYWAY, DON'T YOU DARE COME SEE HER UNTIL SHE'S OUT OF THE HOSPITAL. IF YOU DO...
...I'LL PULL IT OFF!!
PULL OFF WHAT, I WONDER?
ee hee hee.
Just a...
WHO DIED AND MADE YOU TWO QUEENS?!
SHE'S GETTING OUT.
AND SOON.
WHY DON'T YOU PICK HER UP WHEN SHE DOES?

THINK ABOUT IT.

CAN'T YOU CUT EVERYONE A BREAK...

...AND LET HER BELONG TO ALL OF US FOR JUST A LITTLE LONGER?

WHEN THEY DO, YOU'LL HAVE HER ALL TO YOURSELF, ANYWAY.

THEY'RE LETTING HER OUT?

WAIT.

SORRY, BUT I DON'T PLAN ON **EVER** KNOWING THAT.

YOU HAVE NO IDEA HOW I FEEL.

DAMMIT.

shake shake shake

IT'S **NOT** CUTE.

IT'S A CUTE, SELFISH WISH.

SLUMP

...AM I SUPPOSED TO DO TODAY...?

I WAS THINKING...

Was really excited.

SO THEN WHAT...

...THAT I SHOULD TELL SHISHOU ABOUT YESTERDAY.

...I SUPPOSE I FEEL A LITTLE SORRY FOR HIM.

You're hopeless.

What's wrong? You get yelled at again? Yikes.

I'm gonna pound you.

DO YOU REALLY? HUNH.

BUT *THIS* WAS A SHOCK.

CRAP...I SHOULDN'T HAVE SAID ANYTHING TO GIVE HER THE WRONG IDEA LIKE THAT.

HA HA.

AND YET...

WITH ALL HE'S GOING THROUGH...

SIIIIGH

BUT I WOULDN'T DO *SOME* THINGS...

...WE NEED TO TAKE THIS STAND. SIMPLY SAYING HIS NAME REALLY DOES AFFECT HER.

...TO A GIRL I DIDN'T LIKE.

WE REALLY **DO** NEED HIM TO WAIT UNTIL SHE'S OUT OF THE HOSPITAL.

INDEED.

WE DON'T WANT HER TO CRY ON **US**.

AND IF HE CAME, SHE WOULD PROBABLY RUN AWAY BEFORE SHE EVEN PUT ON HER SHOES.

BY THE WAY...

AREN'T YOU GOING, ARISA?

SHE STILL NEEDS HER REST. WE'RE PROTECTING HER.

...

WELL...

YOU KNOW.

YOU SAID IT.

TO SEE KURENO-SAN.

...I'M SURE YOU'RE WORRYING ABOUT PLENTY OF THINGS RIGHT NOW.

BUT IF YOU **CAN** SEE HIM...

...DON'T YOU THINK...

...YOU **SHOULD** SEE HIM?

YOU'RE PROBABLY RIGHT.

I'VE BEEN THINKING, Y'KNOW.

ABOUT KURENO-SAN'S 26 YEARS IN THIS WORLD.

THE THINGS HE ACCOMPLISHED.

THE THINGS HE COULDN'T.

THE THINGS...

...HE LOVED.

BECAUSE OF ME.

I...

I STABBED HIM.

KURENO.

HE'S...

HE'S IN THIS SAME HOSPITAL.

I...

...CHAINED HIM DOWN.

RIGHT NOW.

HEY.

WHAT... SHOULD I...

HE DOESN'T BLAME ME.

BUT KURENO...

I WALKED ALL OVER HIM.

YOU'RE A WOMAN, AREN'T YOU?

KURENO-SAN MENTIONED THAT...

YOU'RE THE ONE, AREN'T YOU?

I THINK I SEE NOW.

...HE HAS TO "BE THERE" FOR.

...HE HAS SOMEONE...

IT WAS SO SIMPLE.

SHE WASN'T THE ONLY REASON...

EVEN MORE SIM- PLE...

...THAN THAT.

...GH.

...I WAS...

UM...

NN...

...UPSET.

KURENO-SAN HAD LIVED 26 YEARS.

AND I'D BARELY BEEN A PART OF THAT.

I'D BEEN POLISHING THE MEMORIES OF THAT **ONE DAY** OVER AND OVER.

I THOUGHT IT WAS KINDA PATHETIC.

AND THAT MORTIFIED ME.

IT WAS THE BASIC FACT...

...THAT I WAS AN OUTSIDER.

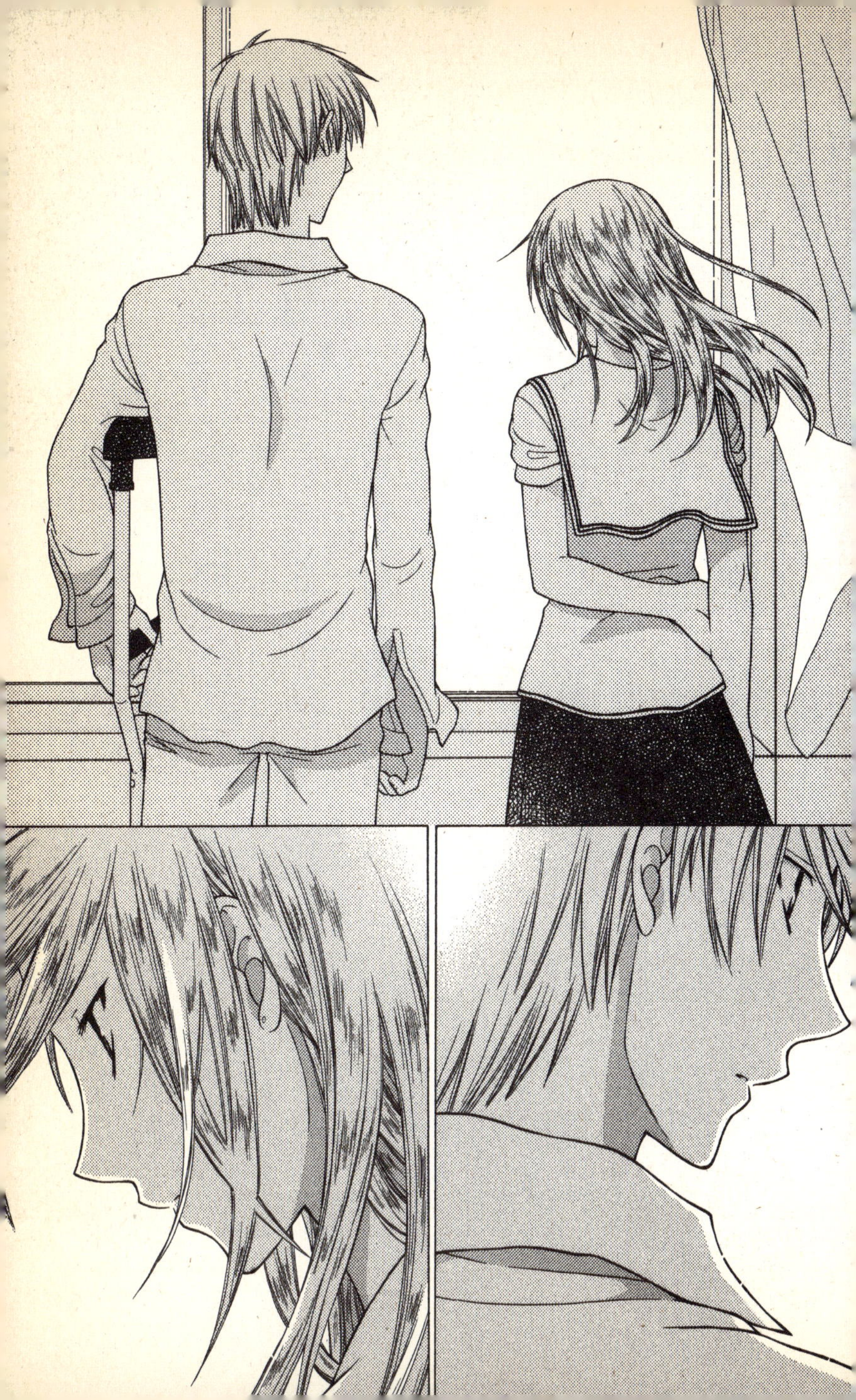

...you would come.

I didn't think...

......

What?

I'm not done. I...

There's still something I have to do.

For Akito.

Why not?

Well...

I don't deserve it.

...

You talked with Akito. Didn't you?

I HAVE TO DISAPPEAR.

IF I'M THERE...

...AKITO WILL NEVER...

...STOP BEING SICK AT HEART.

UNTIL THE END.

UNTIL THE END.

HUNH.

THEN GO.

CAN'T YOU GO ANYWHERE YOU WANT?

ANYWHERE.

I'LL GO ANYWHERE.

HONESTLY.

AND DO Y'KNOW WHY?

HMPH.

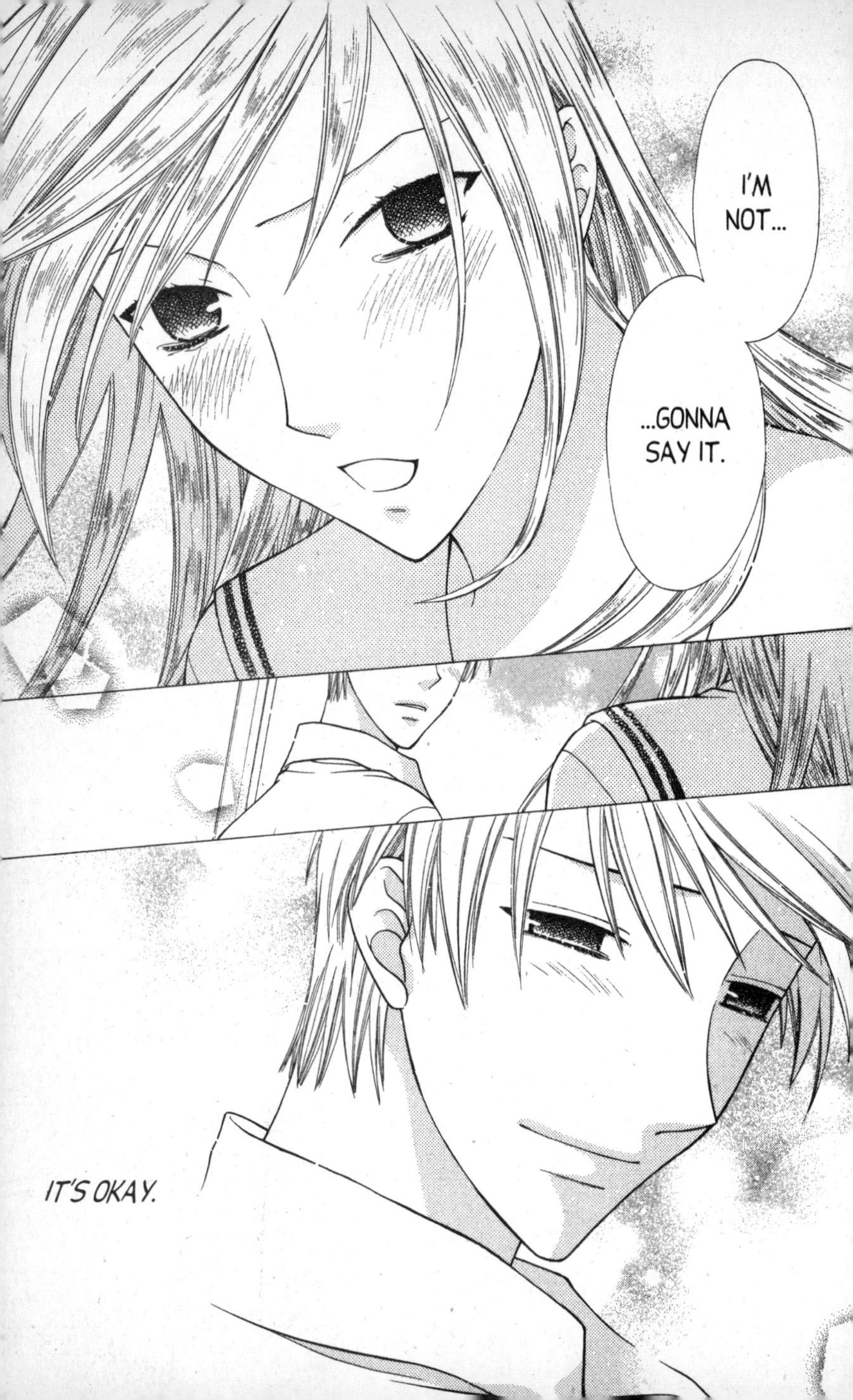
I'M NOT...
...GONNA SAY IT.
IT'S OKAY.

REALLY.

RIGHT NOW, I CAN WAIT.

BUT I'M NOT GONNA BE LEFT OUT OF THINGS.

NOT ANYMORE.

AKITO?

WHAT ARE **YOU** DOING HERE?

WH...

THIS IS SHISHOU'S HOUSE.

DOES IT MATTER?
HUH? WAIT!
I WANNA TALK TO--
WHAP
WE HAVE NOTHING TO TALK ABOUT.
JUST GO ON AND...
...LIVE.
HOWEVER YOU WANT.
....
...HUH?
...
WHAT...
WHAT DO YOU MEAN--
I MEAN WHAT I SAID!
...
I HATE REPEATING MYSELF, OKAY?!
OH...?
CREEEEAK

AA-CHAN.

LEAVING ALREADY?

WHAT ARE YOU DOING HERE?!

HM? OH, HE CAME TO SEE TOHRU-KUN IN THE HOSPITAL, SO I CAME ALONG.

I WANTED TO THANK AZUMA-SAN.

Mwa ha ha ha ha.

THEY'RE LIKE... FRIENDS! GACK!

WHY? IT'S CUTE. YOU SHOULD BE MORE CONFIDENT.

That's not it.

DON'T CALL ME THAT.

I TOLD YOU TO STOP. YOU HAVE TO STOP.

WHA?!

I'LL MAKE MORE TEA.	THANK YOU VERY MUCH.

Sh...!

WHA... THA...!

YOU'RE HERE, KYO.

I THOUGHT I HEARD YOU.

SHE'S LIKE FRIENDS WITH EVERYBODY!

SO YOU WENT TO SEE YOUR FATHER?

I HEAR...

UH... BUH?

HE PROMISED...

...TO DESTROY THE ISOLATED ROOM.

EVEN AKITO-SAN...

...KNOWS ABOUT IT.

BUT STILL.

WE'VE CLEARED ONE OBSTACLE.

WELL.

CORRECTING THE TWISTED ATTITUDES OF YOUR FATHER...

...AND THE PEOPLE AT THE MAIN HOUSE...

...PROBABLY WON'T BE QUITE THAT SIMPLE.

YOU DID WELL.

WHY DON'T YOU HAVE A NICE LONG TALK INSIDE?

YES.

YOU'RE RIGHT.

••••••••••

AFTER THAT...

...A LITTLE TIME PASSED.

AND THEN KURENO-SAN REALLY **DID** LEAVE THE SOHMA HOME.

HE DIDN'T TELL A LOT OF PEOPLE.

HE SAID...

AND HE GOT RID OF ANYTHING HE COULDN'T CARRY WITH HIM.

AND THEN...

...THINGS WOULD WORK OUT BETTER IF HE LEFT THINGS LIKE HE'D NEVER EVEN BEEN THERE.

I KNOW THERE ARE PEOPLE OUT THERE...

...WHO ARE DISGUSTINGLY SELF-CENTERED.

BUT I THINK IT'S OKAY FOR SOME PEOPLE TO BE THE OPPOSITE.

TO ALWAYS PUT THEMSELVES LAST.

...HE SMILED.

THAT'S NOT SO BAD.

ARE YOU SURE... YOU'RE OKAY WITH THIS?

LOOKING FOR A JOB IN THE MIDDLE OF NOWHERE LIKE THIS...

I'M NOT...

WHO CARES IF I'M OKAY? I LIKE IT HERE.

...GOING ANYWHERE.

...WHY?

HM?

I'M NOT GONNA SAY IT.

I WANT YOU...

SAY IT.

...TO SAY IT.

BECAUSE...

Chapter 128

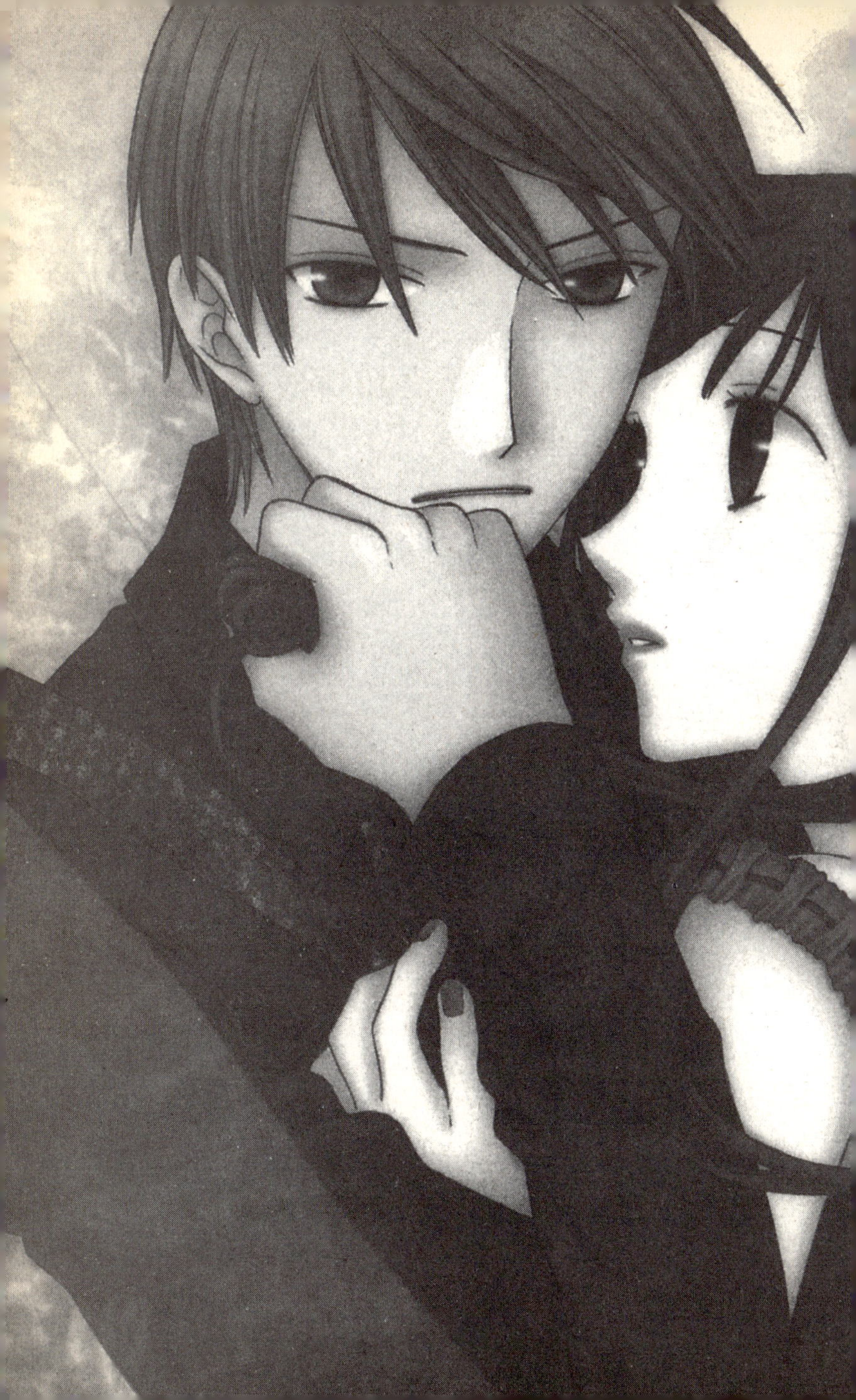

Eep?!

Ha ha ha ha

Now, now. (Since Akito-san is here...) Let's make ourselves comfortable and discuss Kyo's future. (The time for mercy is over.)

Shishou's limiters are off.

...SATCHAN?

SATCHAN!

Gasp!

WHY ARE YOU STANDING IN FRONT OF AKITO'S MANSION?

UM... I'M HERE...

OH.

FOR WHO?

...FOR MORAL SUPPORT.

HIRO.

YOU'RE SO TACT-LESS.

AND THOUGHT-LESS.

BUT YOU ALWAYS WERE.

YOU DON'T HAVE ANY POWER OR JUDGMENT...

...WORTH WRITING HOME ABOUT.

BUT YOU STILL KEEP PUSHING TO GET WHAT ONLY **YOU** WANT.

I...

STILL.

IT WAS NEVER...

THAT QUALITY.

HE WANTS TO TALK?

AKITO WANTS TO TALK?

EAH.

HE SAYS HE WANTS ALL THE ZODIAC TOGETHER.

UH...

AND THAT INCLUDES ME?

I NEVER...

...DISLIKED THAT ABOUT YOU.

There aren't many columns (again) this volume...

He was hard to draw, yet easy to draw.

Kureno

- Kureno, his father, and his mother make his a family of three.
- Since becoming an adult, he hasn't interacted with his parents much.
- And ever since he became the first one to become normal, he avoided interacting with the other members of the Zodiac.
- He may have been the most lonely of all.
- When he first showed up (when he met Uo-chan for the first time at the convenience store), he was holding a lot of bags of snacks because Akito suddenly said she wanted to eat them late at night--so he'd gone to buy them.
- I'm ashamed to say it, but I couldn't make the time to explain that reason in the main story....
- Come to think of it, how does everyone pronounce "Kureno"? With me, it changes whenever I say it.
- Sometimes I'll accent it the same way I do "Momiji," and sometimes it's the same as "Shigure."

YEAH...AT THE MAIN HOUSE.

WHEN?

NEXT WEEK.

.....

I WONDER WHAT WANT TO TALK ABOUT

BUT...

I DUNNO.

HE'S...

...CHANGED.

PROBABLY, ANYWAY.

...CONSIDERING HOW AKITO'S BEEN RECENTLY, IT SHOULD BE OKAY.

YEAH, KIND OF.

Pfft!

...VINDICATING.

SINCE ALL THAT CRAZY CRAP THE OTHER DAY...

...HOW'S SENSEI?

STILL.

IS HE...

Huh? YOU MEAN SHIGURE?

...FIGHTING THESE THINGS BY HIMSELF?

...HE'S BEEN FIGHTING A LOT OF STUFF.

HE'S BEEN OUT OF THE HOUSE A LOT LATELY.

THE "INSIDE" PEOPLE LOOK CONFUSED TOO.

IT'S KINDA...

AAAH...♪

AAAH?

AH?!

Wh...

WHAT? WHAT ABOUT SHIGURE?

NO, I MEAN...

OH.

RIGHT-- I FORGOT.

HEARING THE STUPID VOICE OF AN IDIOT REMINDED ME.

YOU'RE **REALLY** NOT PULLING YOUR PUNCHES THESE DAYS, ARE YOU?

THEY SAY TEASING'S A SIGN OF LOVE.

Right?

I'M SORRY.

I'M **REALLY** SORRY.

FORGET IT--JUST TELL ME WHAT YOU REMEMBERED ALREADY!

HONDA-SAN GETS OUT OF THE HOSPITAL TOMORROW.

Uotani-san told me.

I'M SORRY.

YOU ONLY REMEMBERED NOW?!

I'M REALLY SORRY.

Snicker snicker snicker

Snicker snicker

BY THE WAY.

I WONDER IF THAT MEANS HE'LL BE A LITTLE FREE.

AND IF HE CAN BE WITH HONDA-SAN.

I HEAR THEY'RE GONNA DESTROY...

...THE ISOLATED ROOM.

I DON'T KNOW.
THOSE TWO...
...ARE VERY LUCKY.
STAMP STAMP
SO NOW IT'S OKAY, RIGHT?
OKAY--I KNOW NOW! I KNOW SHE'S GETTING OUT!
STAMP STAMP
GASP WHEEZE GASP
IT'S OKAY FOR ME TO GO PICK HER UP?!
WHEEZE GASP WHEEZE
IT'S OKAY, RIGHT?!
THE PRINCE TOLD YOU ALREADY?
THAT'S NO FUN.
We were too kind.
MAN, YOU'RE ANNOYING! YEAH, IT'S FINE.
Argh!
BUT!

...NNGH.

IT'S...OKAY. I'LL MAKE AN EFFORT.

I mean, she does think you dumped her and all...

YOU CAN'T GET UPSET IF SHE RUNS AWAY FROM YOU.

THEN MAKE SOME EFFORT NOW.

WHAT DO YOU THINK'LL LOOK GOOD ON HER, KYON?

WHAT? CLOTHES?

....

THEY'RE BOTH FINE.

WE THOUGHT WE'D GET HER A PRESENT TO CELEBRATE HER GETTING BETTER.

THIS IS SUPPOSED TO BE ONE OF THE THINGS MEN ARE GOOD FOR.

HEY, HEEEY.

...

UH...

Hey!

MAYBE WE SHOULDN'T DO THIS.

YOU KINDA SOUND LIKE AN OLD MAN.

Wha? REALLY?

I...DON'T REALLY KNOW ABOUT...

...women's clothes.

I'M JEALOUS.

I mean, she thinks you dumped her...

...SHE MIGHT NOT WEAR WHAT WE GET HER.

IF SHE FOUND OUT **YOU** PICKED IT OUT...

MY, HOW TERRIBLE.

STUDENT COUNCIL ROOM

OF THE TWO OF THEM.

PRESIDENT.

...?

HERE. I FINISHED DOING THE TOTALS.

PRESIDENT?

WELL...

I WORKED A LITTLE HARDER THAN USUAL.

...RIGHT.

THANK YOU.

YOU DID THOSE FAST.

HONDA-SAN KNOWS.

THAT KYO'S NOT...

SHE ALREADY KNOWS.

...A NORMAL PERSON.

BUT...

AND SHE HAS FOR A WHILE.

...IN MY CASE...

...MACHI.

...I...

......

I...

IF...

Excuuuuuuuse me.

HAVE YOU SEEN KIMI'S BRUSH?

I HAVEN'T.

Aw! Then where is it?

I...

WHAT ABOUT YOU, YUN-YUN? HAVE YOU SEEN IT?

...

EH, YOU PROBABLY JUST FORGOT IT AT HOME.

Whaaaa?

BUT I ALWAYS CARRY THAT BRUSH WITH ME.

HEY, MACHI? HAVE YOU SEEN IT ANY--

NO.

NOT ONCE.

I HAVE TO TELL HER...

...THAT SHE MAY OR MAY NOT ACCEPT.

...THEN I HAVE TO TELL HER THE ONE THING...

IF I WANT TO STAY WITH HER...

ARE YOU GOING TO HOLD A BANQUET?

SO WHAT'S YOUR PLAN?

I KNOW YOU'RE COLLECTING EVERYONE.

HM.

WELL, AS LONG AS YOU'RE SATISFIED.

THAT'S WHAT'S MOST IMPORTANT, AFTER ALL.

...HEY.

YOU'RE RELIEVED LIKE THE REST OF THEM, AREN'T YOU?

"I'M...

...FREE."

"FROM THE CURSE."

ALL OF IT.

I'M GOING TO "END" IT.

I'LL SAY...

...THE THINGS I SHOULD.

"/..."

IF IT MEANS I'LL BE FREE...

...FROM YOUR BAD BEHAVIOR...

...THEN I WILL BE RELIEVED.

...LEAVE ME AND GO WHEREVER YOU PLEASE.

YOU'LL BE RELEASED FROM ME.

YOU CAN JUST...

BUT THAT FIERY TEMPER OF YOURS WON'T BE CURED OVERNIGHT.

!

I SAID I'VE HAD ENOUGH OF--

I'M NOT "LOOKING DOWN" ON YOU.

...EVERYONE LOOKING DOWN ON ME ANYMORE.

I'VE HAD IT WITH THIS.

I DON'T WANT...

AND HERE.

A GIFT.

I GUESS YOU COULD CALL IT A FAREWELL PRESENT.

I'M TEASING YOU.

BE SURE NOT TO GET THOSE TWO CONFUSED.

...CRAP.

I'M FREAKING OUT MORE BY THE SECOND.

UNLESS... I'M NERVOUS **BECAUSE** I FINALLY GET TO SEE HER?

THIS IS BAD.

FOR SOME REASON...

I WISH HE HADN'T SEEN ME LIKE THIS.

He wanted to give me a hard time again.

HEY.

...I SAID, "HEY"!

...I'M INSANELY NERVOUS.

BWA?!

TWITCH

SHOULDN'T YOU BE GOING SOON?

I THOUGH YOU WERE GOING TO GET HONDA-SAN TODAY.

AND WHEN I FINALLY GET TO SEE HER. CRAP!

WHAT ABOUT YOU?

I'LL PASS.

I HAVE SOMETHING...

I'M SURE YOU DON'T WANT ME GETTING IN THE WAY OF YOUR **LONG-AWAITED REUNION**.

BE-SIDES

I DON'T--

...IMPORTANT TO DO MYSELF.

JUST BE YOURSELF. YOUR STUPID, NORMAL SELF.

DON'T SCREW THIS UP, YEAH?

WHATEVER YOU SAY.

RIGHT.

FOR SOME REASON, I DON'T REALLY KNOW ANYMORE.

WHAT *WAS* BEING NORMAL LIKE?

BE "NORMAL."

MAN.

I JUST...

HOW DID I ALWAYS USED TO TALK TO HER?

AND MORE THAN ANY-THING...

RIGHT NOW, DO I REALLY...

....STILL LIKE HER?

WHAT DO I LIKE ABOUT HER?

AND WHAT DO I LIKE ABOUT *THAT*?

HOW MUCH DO I LIKE IT?

AND WHAT ABOUT... ME?

...WILL SHE STILL ACCEPT ME?

SO MUCH STUFF HAS HAPPENED RECENTLY.

AND SHE THINKS I DUMPED HER.

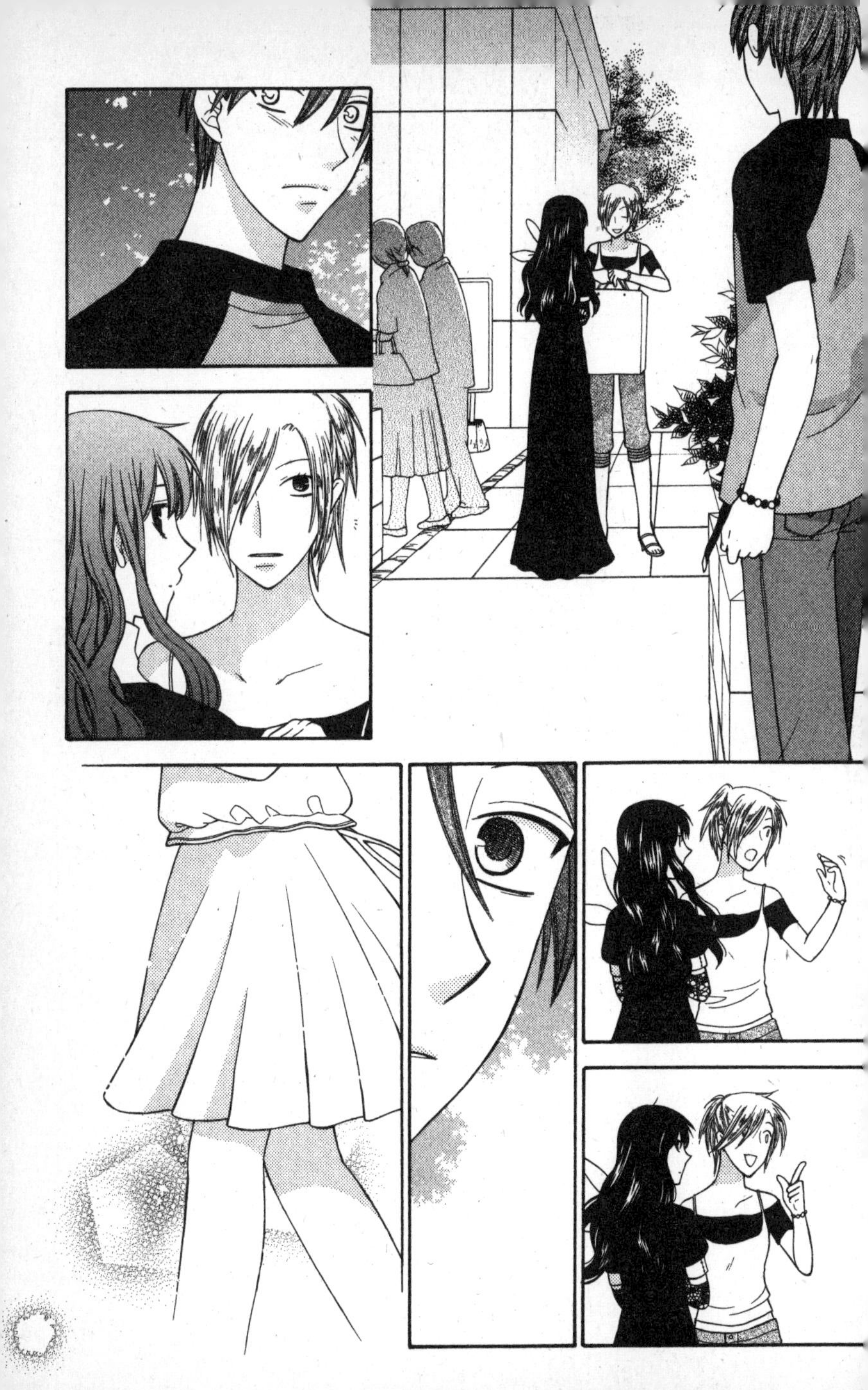

MAN.

NE OF
HAT...

...OH.

...REALLY
MATTERS
AT ALL.

I LOVE HER.

I LOVE HER.

...TOHRU.

I LOVE HER...

...SO MUCH.

I COULD DIE.

CAN I LAUGH AS WELL?

I GUESS ALL HE CAN DO IS LAUGH.

Siiigh

Ah ha ha.

shake shake shake shake

Ha ha ha!

SHE *DID* RUN AWAY.

...G.H.

DAMMIT!

I'M FASTER THAN SHE IS!

I WON'T LET HER GET AWAY THIS TIME.
HI.
MACHI?
GOOD MORNING.
SORRY FOR THE SUDDEN CALL.
WERE YOU ASLEEP?
UM, HEY.
CAN I...
...TALK TO YOU ABOUT SOME-THING TODAY?
......
YEAH.
IT WON'T TAKE LONG.
YEAH...
THERE'S SOME-THING...

...

THE HELL...?

I COULD DIE...

MACHI...

...I REALLY WANT YOU...

...TO HEAR.

I COULD DIE.

...I WANT HER SO BAD.

YOU WERE JUST IN THE HOSPITAL-- STOP RUNNING LIKE A CRAZY PERSON!

Chapter 129

MY FEET...

...TOOK ME AWAY...

...ON THEIR OWN.

AWAY FROM KYO-KUN.

...WHAT I PLANNED AT ALL.

I MADE A DECISION.

THIS WASN'T...

IT'S SO... STRANGE. AND CRAZY.

105

WHEN I SAW HIM...

ONE MORE TIME...

...T...

...I WAS GOING TO SMILE.

TOHRU...

Aaaaaahhh...!

Was he dumped?

I think so.

Did she dump you?

THIS IS DEPRESSING.

DAMMIT.

Haaaaaaaaaaaaaahhhh

BUT IT'S NO USE.

SHUFFLE SHUFFLE

I CAN'T DO IT.

IT'S ALL...

ONCE I UNDERSTOOD THAT...

...FOR ME TO DO.

I KNOW THAT.

THERE'S NOTHING LEFT...

IT'S ALL...

...OVER.

...THEN I...

AND PLEASE, DON'T BE SHY.

JUST LET ME KNOW IF YOU NEED ANYTHING ELSE.

YES! THANK YOU VERY MUCH!

I'M FIT AS A FIDDLE!

Yes!

OF COURSE!

...ARE YOU OKAY?

WE SHOULD TALK ABOUT KYO.

UM...

HE'S...

ACTUALLY...

...SORRY HE....

OH.

I...

IS...!

YOU'RE IN HERE BECAUSE YOU HIT YOUR HEAD!

Really hard!

I'M SORRY!

Ahh!

S-STOP DOING THAT! HEY!

...HURTS.

IT HURTS.

THE SOUND OF HIS NAME...

...IS LIKE A KNIFE IN MY HEART.

IS EVERYTHING ALL RIGHT AT HOME?

IS THE LAUNDRY PILING UP?!

HOW IS... THE CLEANING...

MY CHEST...

I CAN'T...

...BE LIKE THIS.

"I'M DISILL-USIONED."

I'LL ONLY TROUBLE THEM.

I CAN'T KEEP...

...HESI-TATING.

EVERY-ONE...

AND NOT LETTING GO.

...AND KYO-KUN.

I CAN'T DO THAT, NO MATTER WHAT.

SMILE...!

......

DON'T FORGET.

...SMILE.

WHEN YOU SEE HIM ONE MORE TIME...

...YOU HAVE TO SMILE.

...TRAINED MYSELF.

I EVEN...

OR I... THOUGHT I DID.

REALLY.

I CAN'T DO ANYTHING RIGHT.

huff huff huff

IT DOESN'T MATTER.

IT WAS ALL...

I WASN'T LYING WHEN I THOUGHT...

..."THAT'S OKAY."

EVEN IF...

...A WASTED EFFORT.

...I'M NOT...

...BY HIS SIDE.

BUT...

I WASN'T GOING TO LET IT BOTHER ME.

I MADE A DECISION.

I WANT TO BE BY HIS SIDE.
...!
NOT BEING WITH HIM...
.BREAKS Y HEART.
IT BREAKS MY HEART.
P...

I CAN'T CONTROL IT.

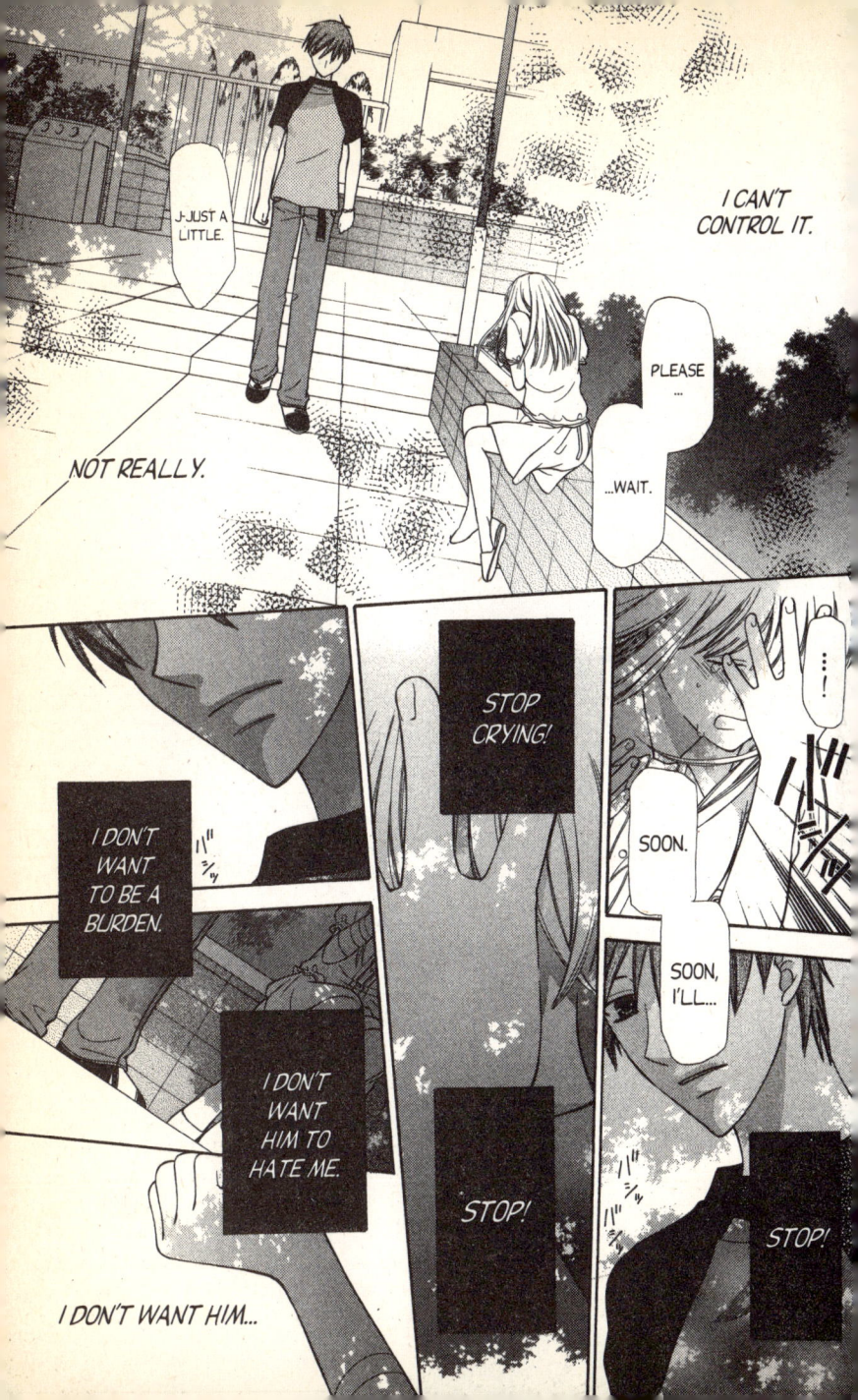

J-JUST A LITTLE.

PLEASE...

...WAIT.

NOT REALLY.

I DON'T WANT TO BE A BURDEN.

STOP CRYING!

SOON.

SOON, I'LL...

I DON'T WANT HIM TO HATE ME.

STOP!

STOP!

I DON'T WANT HIM...

...TO BE DISILLUSIONED ANYMORE.
...
LOOK.
I WAS ONLY...
...THINKING ABOUT MYSELF.

...ALL OF YOUR FEELINGS.

I WAS ONLY THINKING OF MY OWN REGRETS.

I WASN'T CONTROLLING WHAT CAME OUT OF MY MOUTH.

I COMPLETELY IGNORED...

...DOESN'T ALWAYS GIVE YOU THAT LAST CHANCE TO APOLOGIZE.

...SHOULD'VE KNOWN THAT THIS WORLD...

I SHOULD'VE KNOWN BETTER.

ME, OF ALL PEOPLE...

...I NEVER **DID** LEARN.

THAT WOULD BE LIKE...

I CAN'T LET THAT SAME THING HAPPEN AGAIN.

I CAN'T.

B--
I'M SORRY.
FOR MAKING YOU CRY.
I HURT YOU A LOT.
I'M SORRY.
THIS...
...IS THE LAST TIME.
THIS CAN BE THE LAST TIME.
I DON'T NEED ANOTHER ONE.
JUST GIVE ME THIS.
WILL YOU GIVE ME ONE LAST CHANCE?
I WANT...

LISTEN TO ME.
IF I'M GONNA KEEP LIVING...
...I WANT IT TO BE WITH YOU.
...TO BE WITH YOU.
I DON'T WANT ANYONE ELSE.

BECAUSE...

...BECAUSE I LOVE YOU!

...THAT...

...MEAN...

DOES...

......

DOES...

YOU MEAN...

...STAY?

I CAN...

I CAN STAY WITH YOU?

...WITH YOU?

I CAN...

...HOLD...

...YOUR HAND?

AND BE...

I...

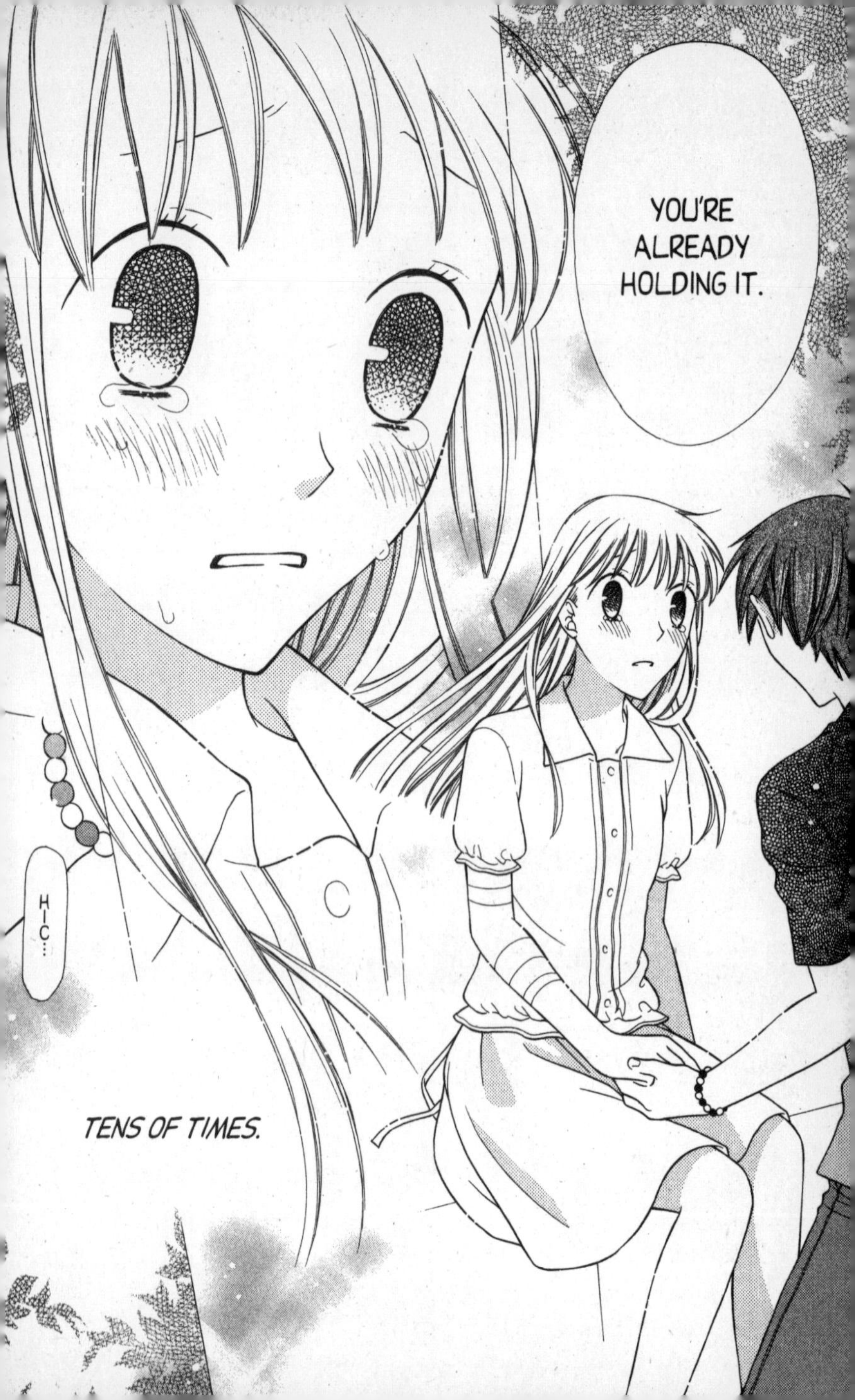
YOU'RE ALREADY HOLDING IT.
HIC...
TENS OF TIMES.

MMMNGH!

THOUSANDS OF TIMES.

HUNDREDS OF TIMES.

NN. NNGH!

I CAN HEAR THE WORDS OVER AND OVER AGAIN.

AND NOW...

...THIS REALLY IS...

...LIKE THE INSIDE OF A DREAM.

KYO-KUN.

WHAT?!

YOU KNOW THIS IS OUR SECOND TIME, RIGHT?

...BY THE WAY.

B...
WHAT?!
WHEN?!
HUH?!
She was unconscious.
SO SHE REALLY DOESN'T REMEMBER.
Now it's like I attacked her in her sleep.
I-I'M SORRY. UM, WHEN DID YOU...
TRY TO REMEMBER, OKAY?
IF YOU REALLY CAN'T...
...THAT'S PRETTY DEPRESS-ING, RIGHT?
OH!
R-RIGHT!

CAN I...
...HOLD YOU?
I'LL LOSE HUMAN FORM AFTER-WARD.
I KNOW.
...I'M SURE THERE'LL BE TIMES THAT I'LL MAKE YOU SUFFER.
IF WE'RE TOGETHER...
...
THE CURSE IS STILL BETWEEN US.
KYO-KUN.
DIDN'T YOU KNOW?
KYO-KUN...
...I REALLY DO LOVE YOU.

...IS INVINCIBLE.

I REALLY, REALLY DO.

OKAY, KYO-KUN?

AND THAT FEELING...

HEH HEH!

THERE'S NOTHING FOR ME TO BE SCARED OF.

...I'M INVINCIBLE TOO.

UH... REALLY?

RIGHT?

THEN I GUESS...

AS LONG AS I HAVE YOU!

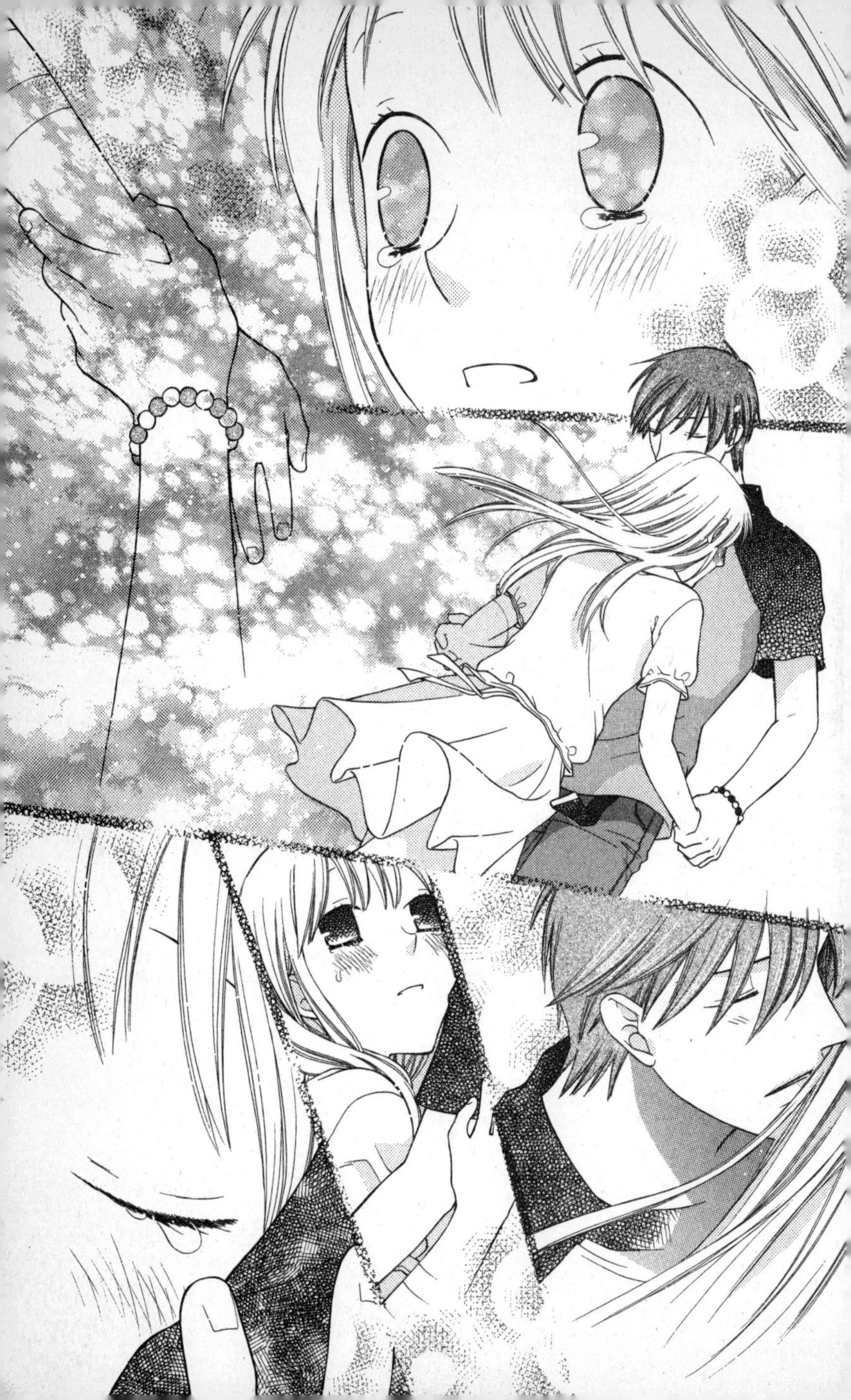

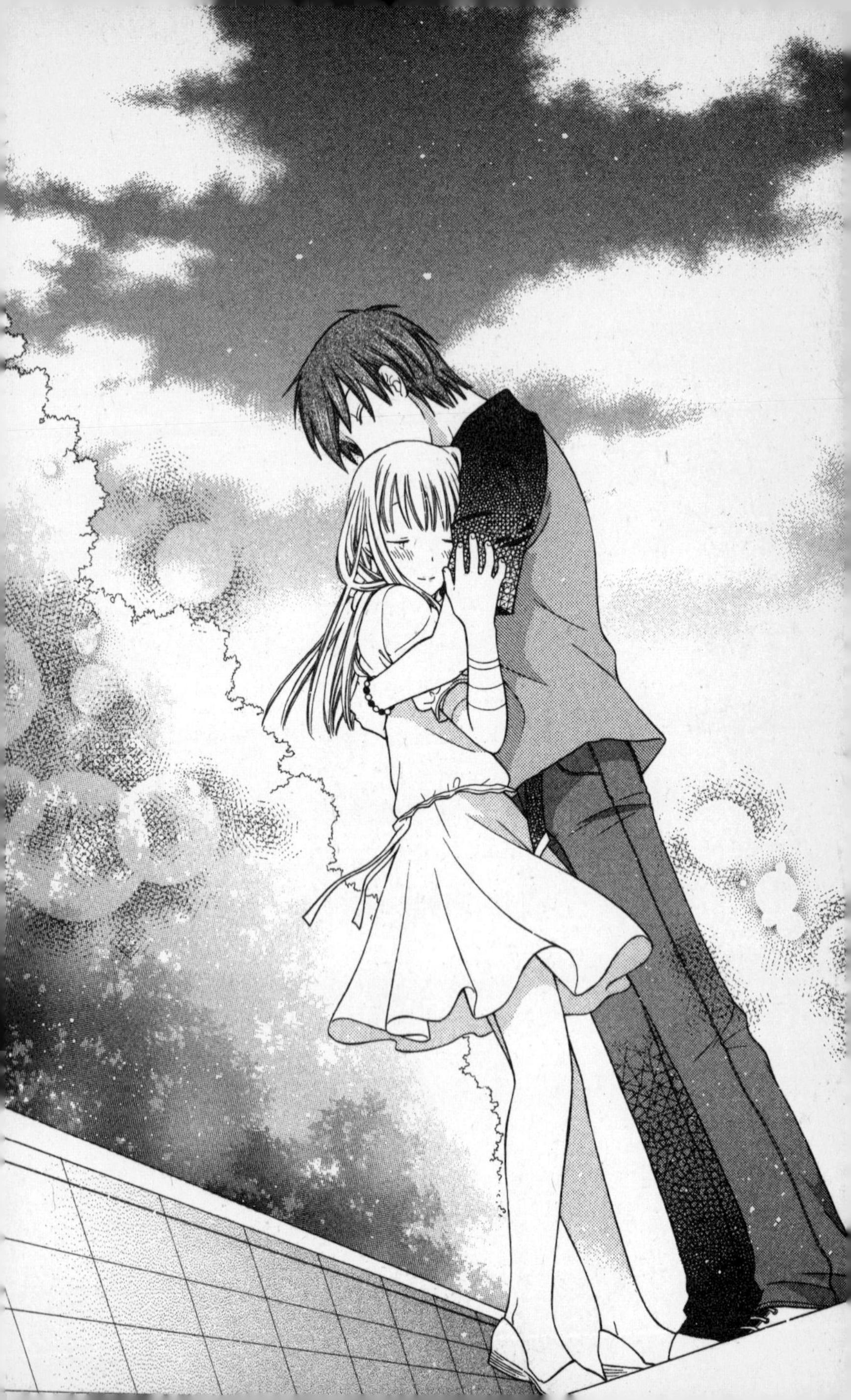

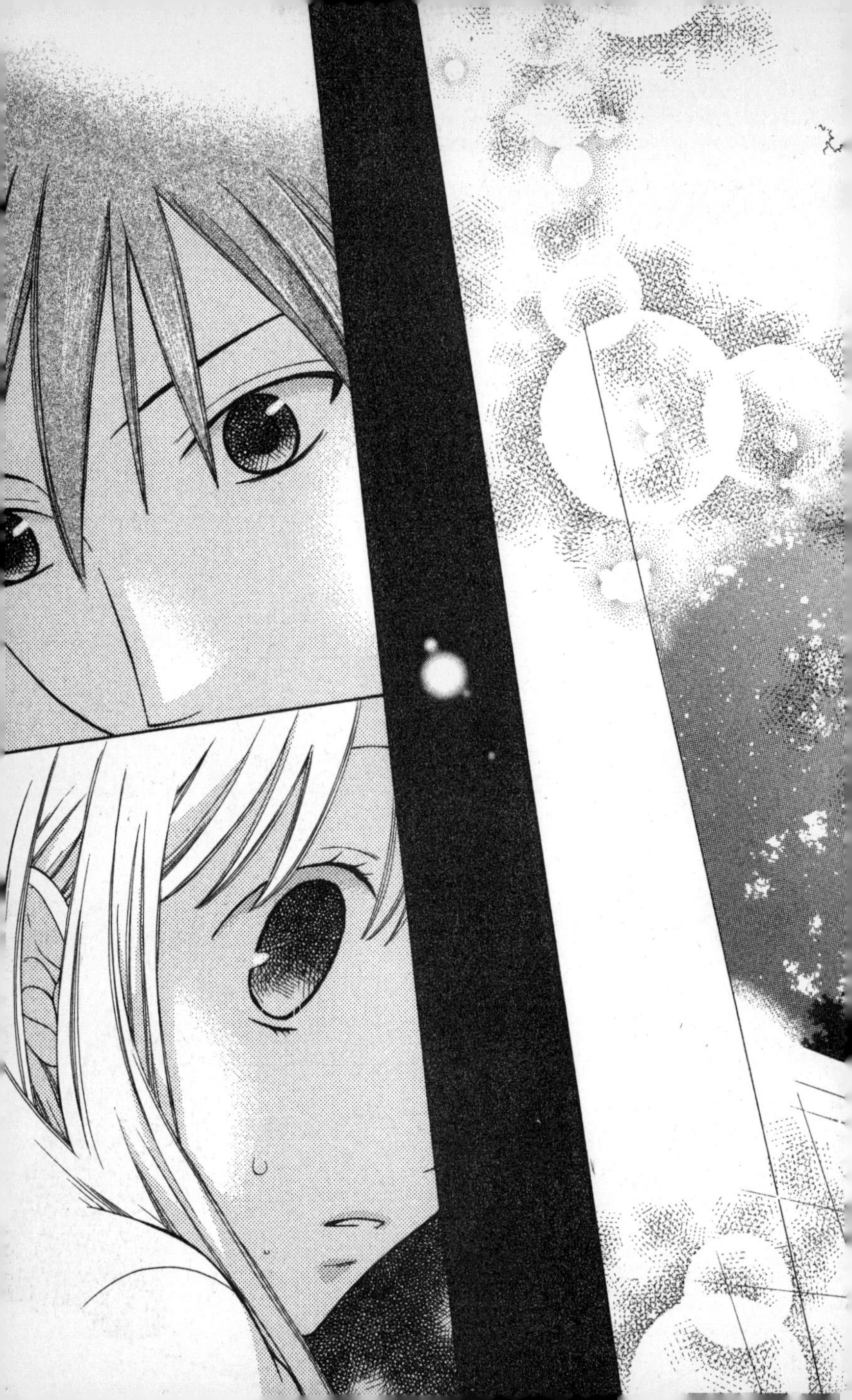

GOODBYE.

Chapter 130

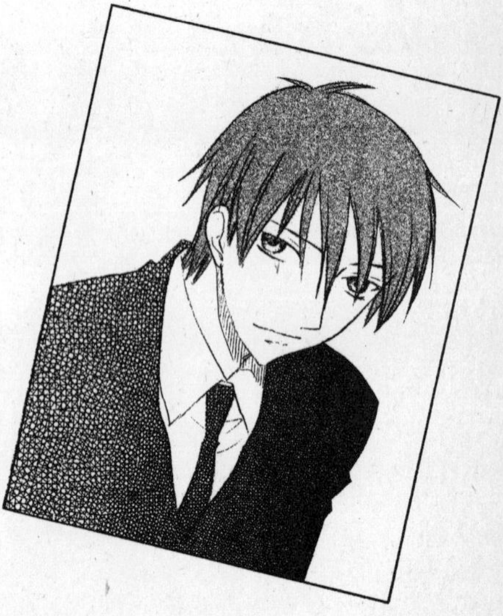

I WAS JEALOUS OF YOU.

I WAS JEALOUS.

I'M SERIOUS.

YOU WERE SO MUCH...

...PRETTIER THAN ME.

: : :

"DON'T DIVIDE THINGS INTO CATEGORIES."

LIKE 'PRETTY.'

YOU SAY...

...THAT I'M PRETTY, AKITO-SAN?

THEN YOU'RE PRETTY TOO.

WHEN YOU DO THAT...

...YOU JUST USE THEM TO SEPARATE YOURSELF OUT.

I'M...

I'M NOT... PRETTY.

PLEASE.

I WAS TRYING TO DESTROY...

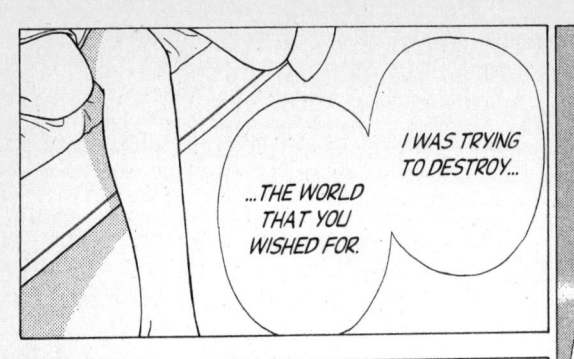

...THE WORLD THAT YOU WISHED FOR.

YOU CRIED...

...BECAUSE YOU WERE LONELY AND SCARED.

IT DOESN'T MATTER IF IT WAS RIGHT OR WRONG.

YOU WERE PAINFULLY INNOCENT.

IT DOESN'T CHANGE THE FACT...

...THAT I HURT YOU A LOT, AKITO-SAN.

SO PURE.

BUT...

EVEN SO...

KYO...
KUN?

...

GOODBYE.

IT...

IT'S...

...OKAY NOW, RIGHT...?

...

...OKAY.

IT'S...

FATHER.

I CAN JUST BE...ME.

I DON'T HAVE TO BE "GOD" ANYMORE.

..."SPECIAL" ANYMORE.

I DON'T HAVE...

...TO BE...

RIGHT...?

I KNOW WHAT I DON'T HAVE.

I-I CAN START DOWN...

...MY OWN PATH.

......

I...

"I" AM...

SO HURT.

SO SCARED!

I KNOW I DON'T HAVE ANYTHING REDEEMING ABOUT ME, BUT...!

GOODBYE.

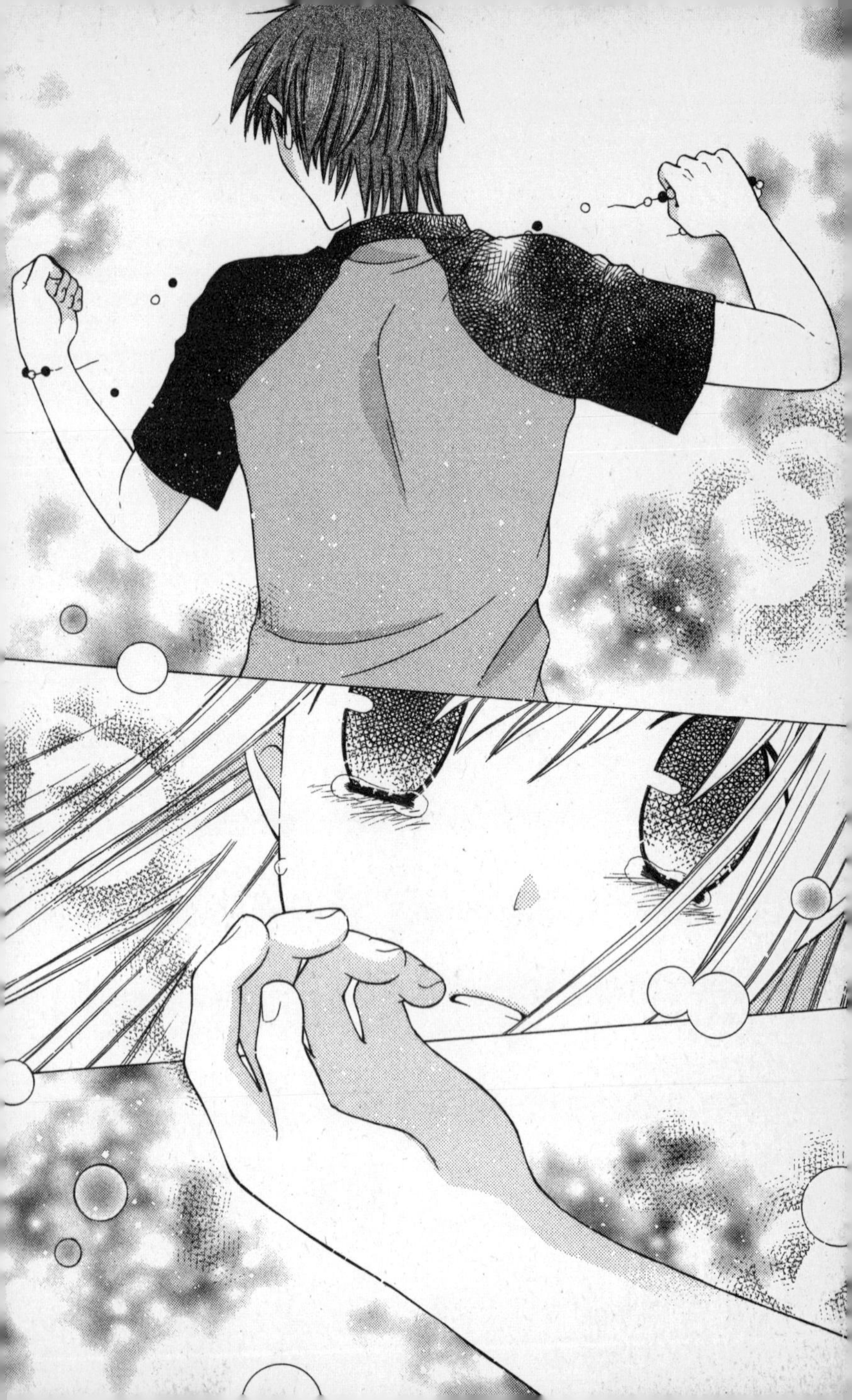

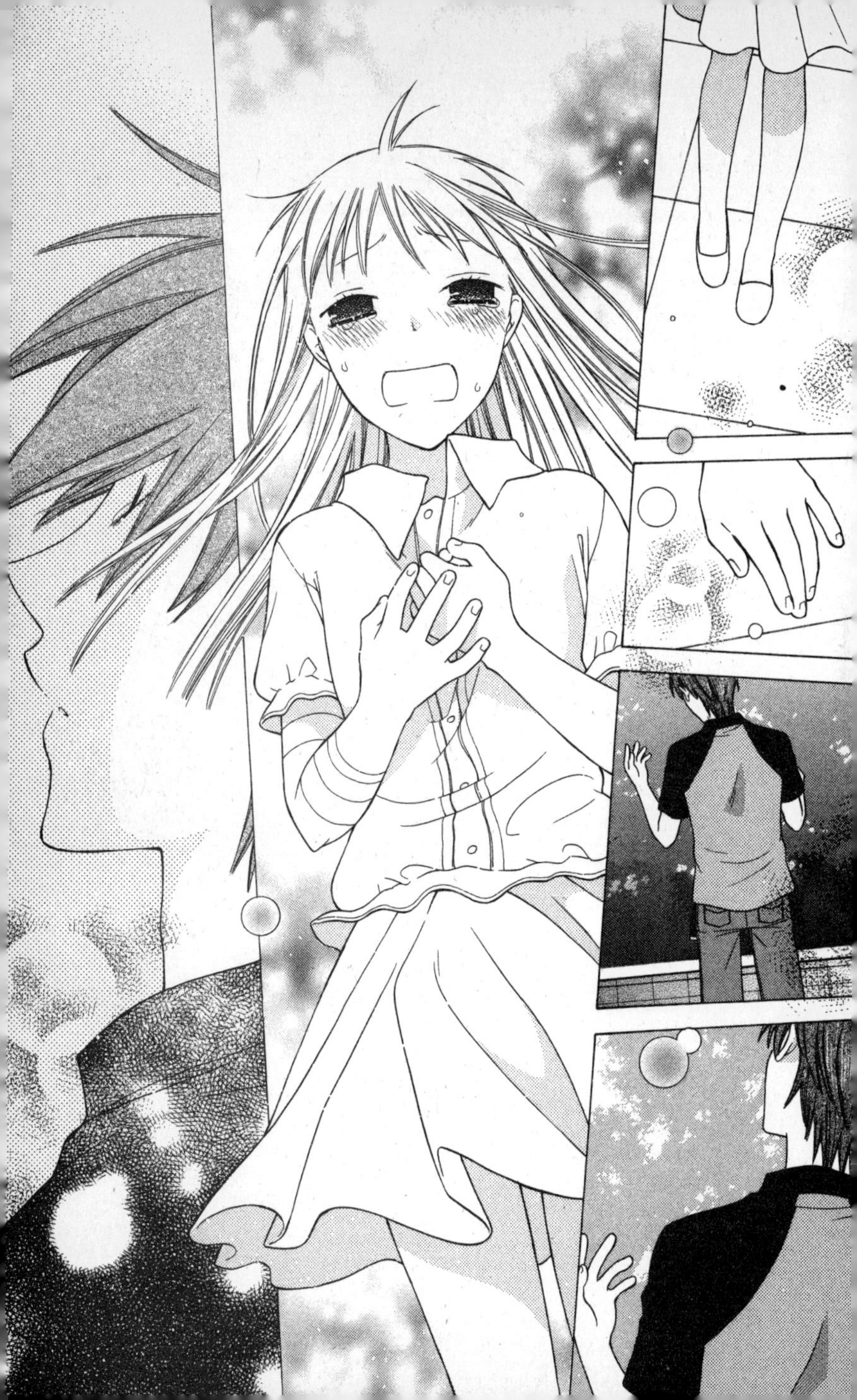

GOODBYE.

COMING!

WHAT IS IT? MORE TEA?

MI-NE...

LUNCH IS ALMOST READY, BY THE WA--

WHAT KIND WOULD YOU LIKE?

MINE.

...?

MA...

MI-NE.

...TO LOVE YOU.

I WISHED...

I WAS BORN FOR A REASON.

WH... WHAT'S WRONG?!

RITSU?!

ARE YOU ALL RIGHT?! YOU'RE NOT HURT, ARE YOU?!

GOOD-BYE.

EVERY-ONE.

CRRRASH

AND NOW...

...I CAN FINALLY TELL YOU THAT.

VERY LONELY.

IT'S LONELY TO SAY GOODBYE.

"BEGINNINGS HAPPEN BECAUSE THERE ARE ENDINGS."

"PARTINGS ARE THE BEGINNINGS OF NEW MEETINGS."

NO.

NOT NOW.

I DON'T WANT TO HEAR...

...THOSE SIMPLE CLICHÉS.
......
HUNH.
IN A WAY...
...THIS IS PRETTY DEPRESSING.

MAYBE THERE'S NOTHING WE CAN DO ABOUT THIS.

BUT AT LEAST, FOR NOW...

PLEASE.

CRY WITH ME.

...CRY WITH ME.

LIKE YOUR ENTIRE BODY...

...IS SCREAMING AT THE SKY.

LIKE IT'S RAGING AGAINST THE WORLD.

I LOST SOMETHING.

AND I DON'T HAVE A SINGLE GUARANTEE.

THE FEAR OF LIVING IN THIS WORLD AGAIN AFTER THAT...

...

...

I HAVE ONLY A SHRED OF HOPE TO SUSTAIN ME.

...HUH.

SO I WANT YOU, AT LEAST...

SO THIS...

...IS HOW IT FEELS.

...TO CRY.

CRY.

CRY WITH ME.

LIKE THE DAY YOU WERE FIRST BORN INTO THIS WORLD.

BUT DESPITE ALL THAT, AKITO-SAN.

...THAT I CAN BE YOUR FRIEND.

PLEASE?

I STILL HOPE...

"...TO BECOME FRIENDS."

...TO BELIEVE IN THEM AFTER THE FACT.

YOU NEVER GIVE UP, DO YOU?

"MEETINGS."

"BEGINNINGS."

IT'S NOT TOO LATE...

SMILE.

...WEIRD, SOMEHOW.

I FEEL...

HUH?

......

MAYBE I'M JUST NERVOUS?

BUT...

PRESIDENT!

I-I'M SORRY!

I'M LATE, AREN'T I?

I'M SORRY FOR MAKING YOU WAIT.

YOU SAID IT WAS IMPORTANT, SO...	I'M SORRY FOR THE SHORT NOTICE.
IT'S FINE.	

IT'S OKAY-- YOU'RE NOT LATE.

DID YOU RUN HERE?

Huh?

NO! I DIDN'T... RUN.

THERE'S SOMETHING I HAVE TO...

......

YEAH.

...TELL...

YOU'RE THE LAST.

THANK YOU.

FOR KEEPING...

PRES...

IS SOMETHING WRONG?

PRESIDENT?

...THE VERY DISTANT...

...PROMISE.

PRESIDENT?

THANK YOU.

AND GOODBYE.

Chapter 131

ONCE UPON A TIME, IN A PARTICULAR PLACE...

...THERE LIVED A PERSON.

THE PERSON WAS ALONE.

FOR A LONG, LONG TIME.

AFTER LEAVING THE MOUNTAIN...

...THIS PERSON LEARNED THAT MANY, MANY PEOPLE LIVED BELOW IT.

BUT THE PERSON WAS STILL ALONE.

EVEN WITH A THOUSAND POWERS AND A THOUSAND LIVES...

...AND A THOUSAND MEMORIES.

THE PERSON LEARNED THAT SUCH THINGS WERE DIFFERENT FROM WHAT MOST OTHER PEOPLE HAD.

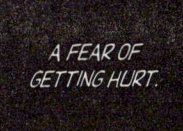

ONE DAY...

...A CAT CAME TO VISIT.

THE PERSON WAS BEWILDERED BY THE SUDDEN VISITOR.

THE CAT BOWED HIS HEAD REVERENTLY.

"I HAVE HUMBLY WATCHED YOU FOR A LONG TIME," HE SAID.

...THE PERSON WAS AFRAID...

...OF BEING DIFFERENT FROM OTHERS.

AND THUS.

...DEVELOPED A FEAR OF OTHER PEOPLE.

A FEAR OF GETTING HURT.

DESPITE HAVING MANY POWERS...

"YOU ARE A VERY MYSTERIOUS PERSON."

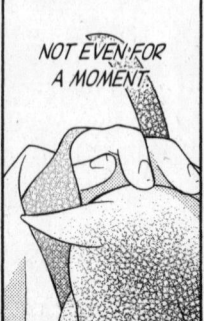

"I CANNOT STOP BEING ATTRACTED TO YOU."

"I AM MERELY A STRAY CAT...

..BUT PLEASE LET ME BE BY YOUR SIDE."

FROM THAT TIME ON...

"PLEASE, LORD GOD."

AND THAT MADE GOD VERY, VERY HAPPY.

NOT EVEN FOR A MOMENT.

...THE CAT KEPT HIS PROMISE.

HE NEVER LEFT GOD'S SIDE.

SUDDENLY, GOD HAD AN IDEA.

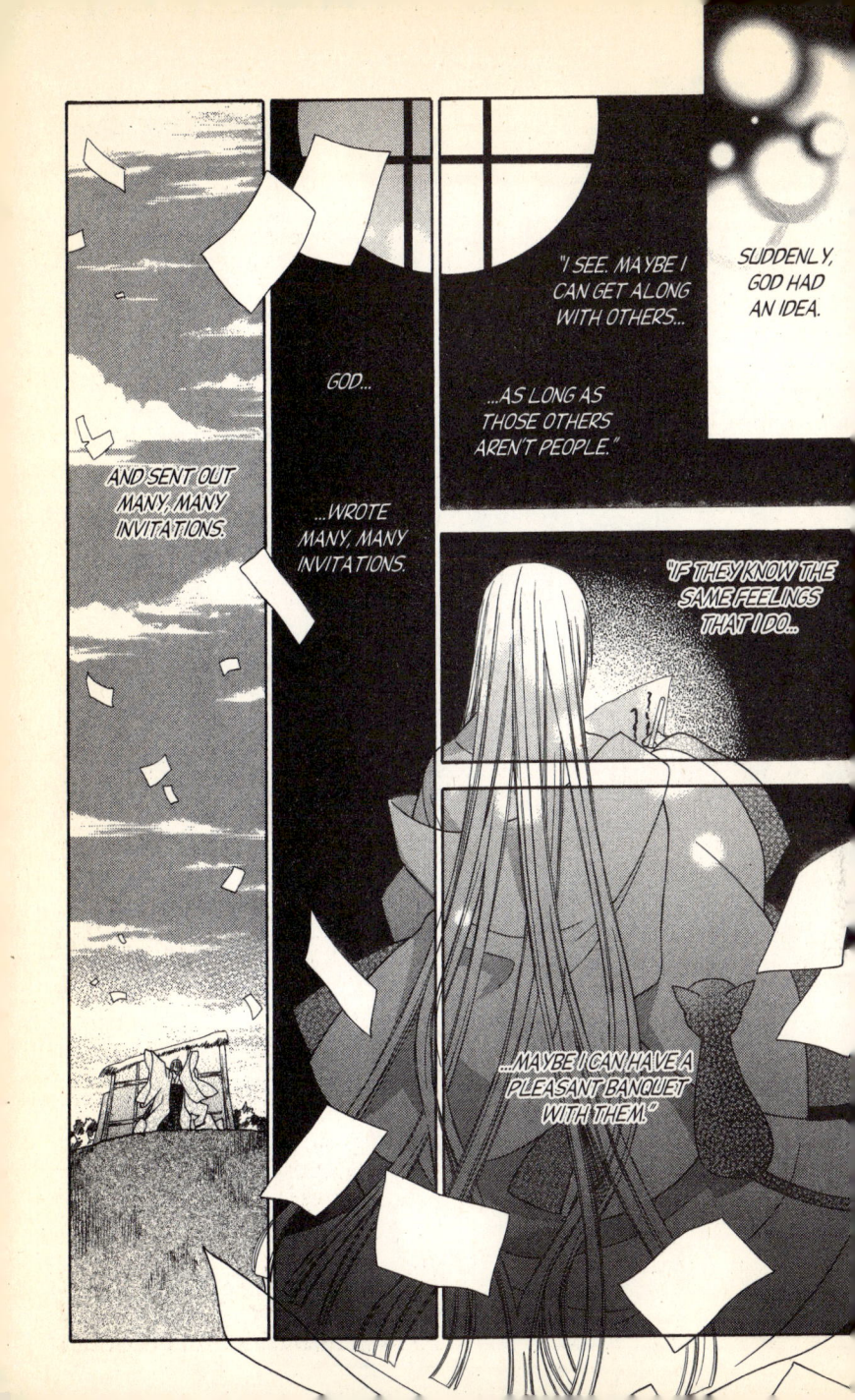

"I SEE. MAYBE I CAN GET ALONG WITH OTHERS...

...AS LONG AS THOSE OTHERS AREN'T PEOPLE."

GOD...

"IF THEY KNOW THE SAME FEELINGS THAT I DO...

...WROTE MANY, MANY INVITATIONS.

...MAYBE I CAN HAVE A PLEASANT BANQUET WITH THEM."

AND SENT OUT MANY, MANY INVITATIONS.

GOD WAS THUS SURROUNDED BY THIRTEEN ANIMALS IN ALL.

THEY ALL HELD A BANQUET EVERY NIGHT THE MOON SPARKLED.

...EY SANG, AND DANCED...

...AND LAUGHED TOGETHER.

AS A RESULT...

...TWELVE ANIMALS CAME TO SEE GOD.

BUT ONE NIGHT...

...THE CAT COLLAPSED.

NOTHING COULD BE DONE. HIS LIFE HAD RUN OUT.

THEY ALL CRIED.

IT MADE THEM REALIZE...

AND GOD, TOO, LAUGHED OUT LOUD FOR THE FIRST TIME.

THE MOON QUIETLY WATCHED OVER...

...THE INHUMAN BANQUET.

...THAT SOMEDAY, EVERYONE WOULD DIE.

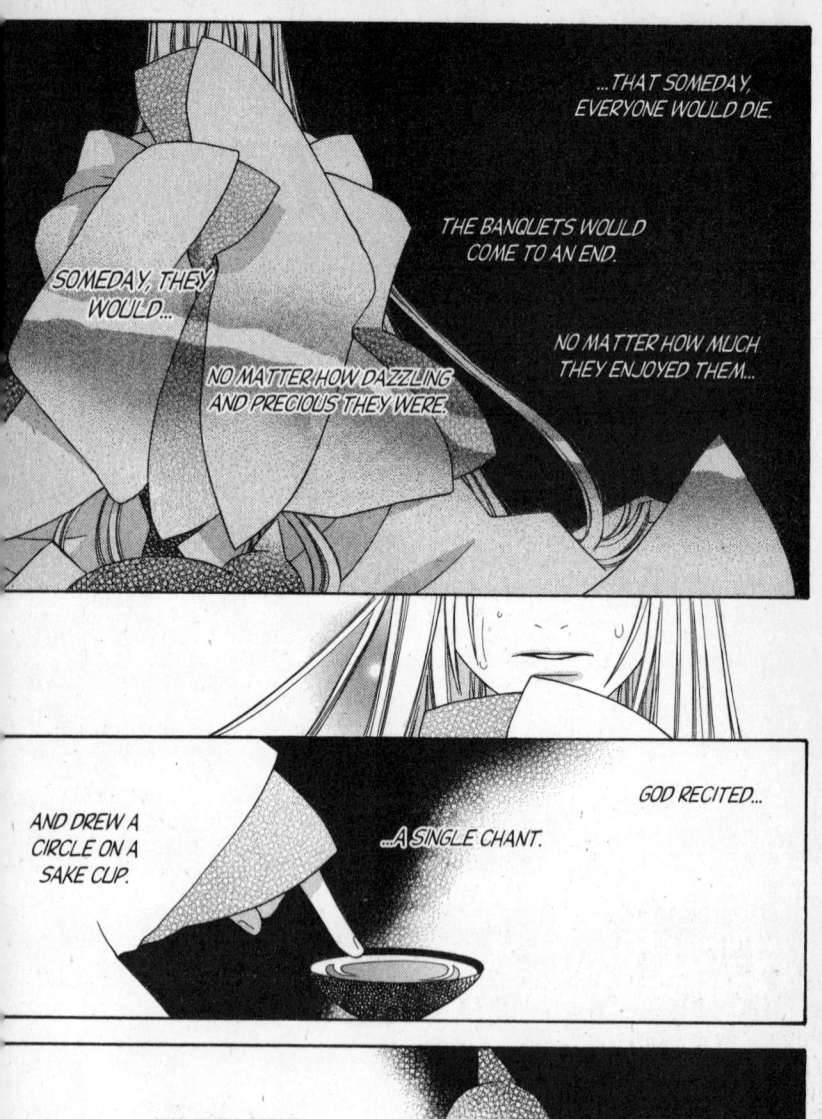

THE BANQUETS WOULD COME TO AN END.

SOMEDAY, THEY WOULD...

NO MATTER HOW MUCH THEY ENJOYED THEM...

NO MATTER HOW DAZZLING AND PRECIOUS THEY WERE.

GOD RECITED...

...A SINGLE CHANT.

AND DREW A CIRCLE ON A SAKE CUP.

GOD MADE THE CAT DRINK.

AND THEN SPOKE TO EVERYONE.

"OUR BOND," GOD SAID.

"HOWEVER MANY TIMES WE DIE."

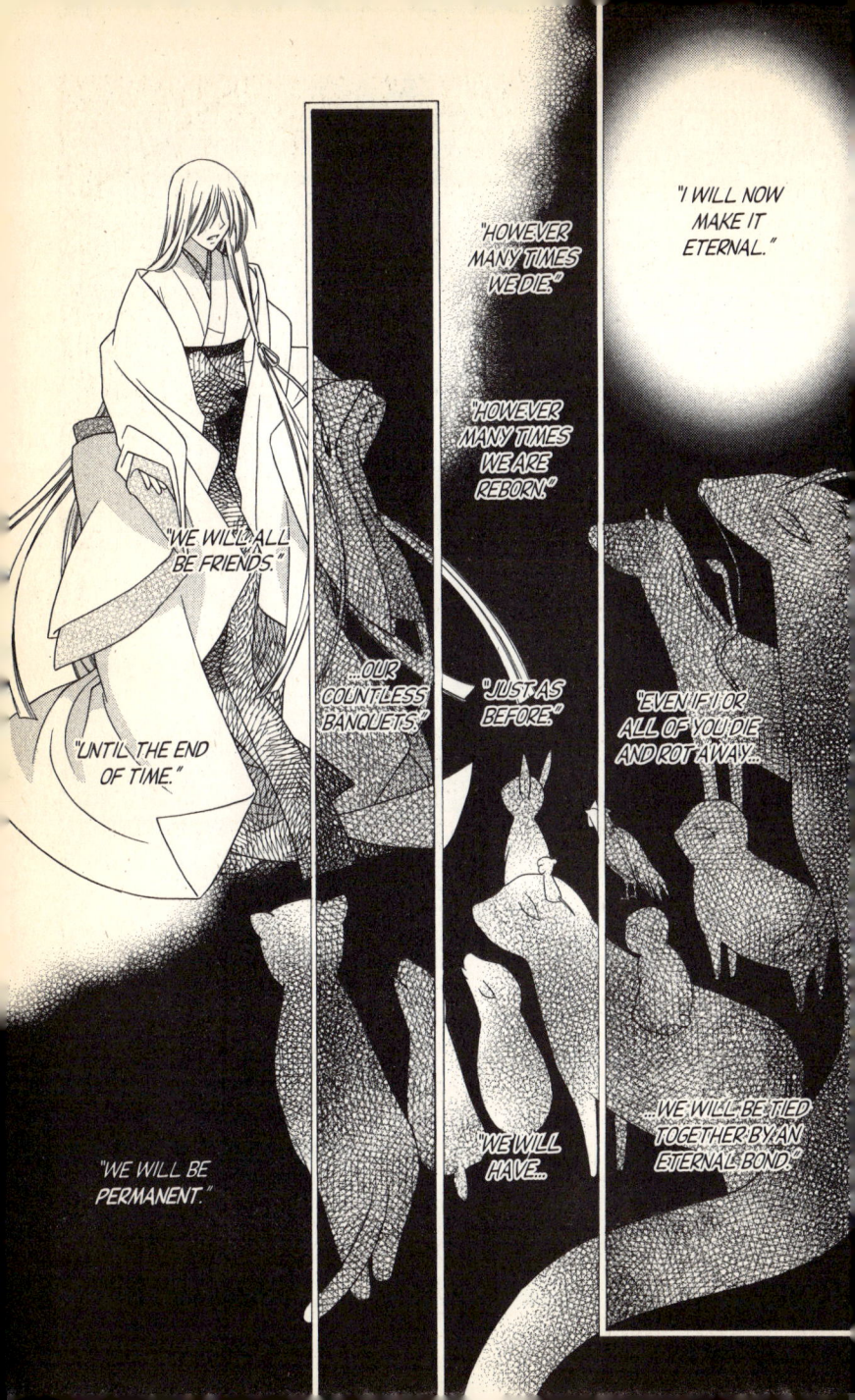

"I WILL NOW MAKE IT ETERNAL."

"HOWEVER MANY TIMES WE ARE REBORN."

"WE WILL ALL BE FRIENDS."

"...OUR COUNTLESS BANQUETS."

"JUST AS BEFORE."

"EVEN IF I OR ALL OF YOU DIE AND ROT AWAY..."

"UNTIL THE END OF TIME."

"WE WILL HAVE..."

"...WE WILL BE TIED TOGETHER BY AN ETERNAL BOND."

"WE WILL BE PERMANENT."

ALL IN ORDER...

...THEY SHARED THE DRINK OF THEIR VOW.

NEXT, THE OX.

NEXT, THE TIGER.

NEXT, THE RABBIT.

EVERYONE NODDED EMPHATICALLY.

THE RAT WAS THE FIRST TO DRINK.

"MY LORD GOD."

...THE CAT STARTED TO CRY, HIS BREATH FAINT.

WHEN FINALLY THE BOAR DRANK...

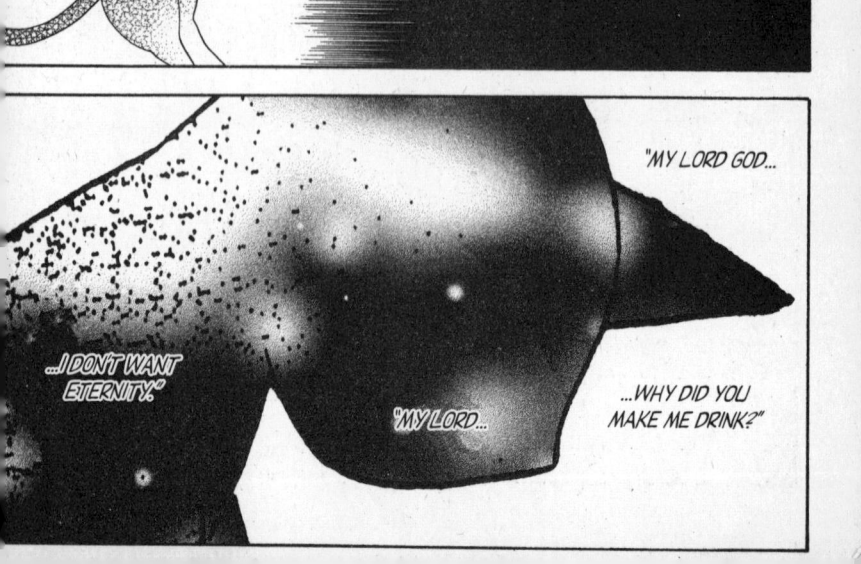

"MY LORD GOD...

...I DON'T WANT ETERNITY."

"MY LORD...

...WHY DID YOU MAKE ME DRINK?"

IT DEVASTATED THEM.

THEY SCOLDED AND ADMONISHED THE CAT.

TO GOD AND THE OTHERS...

"I DON'T NEED PERMANENCE."

THOSE WORDS...

"MY LORD GOD, MY LORD GOD. I KNOW IT'S FRIGHTENING...

EVEN SO, THE CAT SPOKE.

...THEY WERE WORDS OF REJECTION.

...BUT LET US ACCEPT THAT THINGS END."

"I KNOW IT'S SAD...

...WERE UNEXPECTED.

...BUT LET US ACCEPT THAT LIVES DEPART."

THE CAT TWITCHED HIS TAIL ONE LAST TIME AND DIED.

"NEXT TIME, I DON'T WANT TO MEET YOU WITH ONLY THOSE OF US HERE."

"I WANT TO MEET YOU WHILE YOU'RE SMILING...

...WITHIN A RING OF PEOPLE."

"...I DON'T WANT TO ONLY SEE YOU IN THE MOONLIGHT."

"I WANT TO SEE YOU SMILING UNDER THE LIGHT OF THE SUN AS WELL."

"MY LORD GOD, I KNOW IT WAS ONLY FOR A SHORT TIME."

"BUT I WAS HAPPY TO BE WITH YOU."

"IF ONE MORE TIME...

...WE BOTH DIE AND ARE REBORN...

...AND IF WE MEET AGAIN...

SOME TIME AFTER THAT, ONE AFTER ANOTHER...

...THE OTHERS DIED.

FINALLY, AFTER THE DRAGON DIED...

THEY WERE FILLED WITH THE SENSE THAT THE CAT HAD BETRAYED THEM.

...GOD WAS LEFT ALL ALONE AGAIN.

BUT NO ONE CARED ABOUT THE CAT ANYMORE.

"WE'LL HOLD OUR BANQUETS."

"ONCE AGAIN...

...AND AS MANY TIMES AS WE WANT."

"FOR AS LONG AS WE WISH."

AND THEN ANOTHER DAY CAME.

A DAY WHEN EVEN GOD DIED.

BUT GOD WASN'T AFRAID.

BECAUSE GOD WAS SUPPORTED BY THE PROMISE MADE WITH THE OTHERS.

"AGAIN."

"WITHOUT CHANGING."

"I MAY BE SAD AND ALONE NOW...

EVERYONE HAS FORGOTTEN...

...THEIR FIRST MEMORIES.

...FROM LONG, LONG AGO.

THEIR FIRST PROMISE.

...BUT EVERYONE IS WAITING ON THE OTHER SIDE OF OUR PROMISE."

NOW IT'S A TALE...

S-SORRY.

SORRY FOR SUDDENLY...

IT'S JUST...

......

PRESIDENT...?

...FOR A VERY LONG TIME.

TO SOMEONE WHO WAS WITH ME...

I JUST SAID GOODBYE.

BEING TOGETHER WAS REALLY... DIFFICULT.

WE WERE TOGETHER, BUT...

IT WAS MORE LIKE A BURDEN THAN A BLESSING.

BUT NOW...

...THAT WE'RE APART...

DAMMIT.

......!

IT'S NOT... FAIR OF ME TO BE LIKE THIS.

"GOODBYE."

BUT IN EXCHANGE...

...I WAS GIVEN...

..."FREEDOM."

...NO.

I WON'T.

I'M SURE OF IT.

UM. YOU WON'T EVER...

...SEE THIS PERSON AGAIN?

I'M SORRY.

...TO TELL YOU.

...WHAT I WANTED...

THIS ISN'T EXACTLY...

I'M NOT MAKING ANY SENSE, AM I?

YOU MUST BE CONFUSED.

RIGHT NOW, THIS IS ENOUGH.

BUT WHATEVER.

WHAT?

WAIT.

THERE'S SOME THING...

...I WANTED...

...TO ASK YOU TOO.

...

ER...

I...

ACTU- ALLY...

IS IT OKAY...

...IF I CALL YOU BY YOUR NAME?

...

OF COURSE IT'S OKAY.

SAY IT.

YU...

...KI.

ONE MORE TIME.

Y...

YUKI.

AS MANY TIMES AS YOU WANT.

THAT FIRST...

...PROMISE.

AT WHAT POINT...

...DID IT BECOME A CURSE?

WHEN DID IT CHANGE...

...INTO A BURDEN?

THOSE DAYS THAT
WERE SO HAPPY.

THE DAYS THAT
WERE SO HARD
TO PART WITH.

...SUPPOSED TO BE LOVE THERE.

THERE WAS...

TIME PASSED.

AND IT BECAME NOTHING BUT PAIN.

PEOPLE CHANGED.

...TO ALL OF YOU...

...WHO CONTINUED TO SHOULDER THAT EXHAUSTED PROMISE...

I'M SORRY.

BUT...

THE PROMISE THAT LOST ITS ORIGINAL FORM.

THE MOST IMPORTANT THING I WANT TO TELL YOU...

I'M SORRY.

...IS THANK YOU.

THANK YOU.

A STORY OF LONG, LONG AGO.

THE FIRST MEMORIES THAT EVERYONE FORGOT.

IT WASN'T UNTIL MUCH...

...MUCH...

...MUCH LATER...

...THAT THE CAT'S WISH WAS FINALLY GRANTED.

To Be Concluded in Volume 23

I feel so grateful!

Harada-sama, Araki-sama, Mother-sama, Editor-sama
And everyone who reads and supports this manga.

And lastly, to you know who.

This has been **Natsuki Takaya**.

Next time in...

Fruits Basket

The #1 selling shojo manga in America!

23

Natsuki Takaya

The Journey's End...

Curses have broken and the eternal banquet has finally come to a close. But there are still some loose ends to be wrapped up before the last page of Fruits Basket arrives! How will each of the members of the Zodiac deal with their newfound freedom? Can forgiveness come in the wake of Akito's past actions, and a new surprising revelation?

Fruits Basket Volume 23
Available July 2009

Fans Basket

Fans Basket is back thanks to awesome intern Stephanie Trautwein from Los Angeles. She picked out a great batch of art to highlight and wrote some inspired comments. Thanks for all your help, Stephanie! And of course, thanks to all the fans who keep sending us their wonderful work. To properly thank you all, we are sending out postcards to all of you who provided addresses. And to those who we couldn't reach, please know that we appreciate you so much. Thank you for helping make Fruits Basket the phenomenon that it is!

And so we can continue to appreciate all the great fan art you guys provide, TOKYOPOP is starting something new. From now on, please do NOT send any more fan art to our office. Huh? What? Relax! What we want instead is for you to upload the images to our website! This way, everyone can appreciate your work even after volume 23 is published. Check the end of this section for exactly what to do. Fruits Basket Forever!

- Alexis Kirsch, Editor

Jessica Lin
Age 13
Lexington, MA

I have to tell you, I wish I could draw this well when I was thirteen—or even now, for that matter! This artwork is so darling; Akito and Yuki's hair is shaped with great grace and the eyes, especially Yuki's, show great emotion. The question on Yuki's right side begs to be thought about. Is it love or is it hate? I do not think I understand the answer yet—do you?

**Alexander Oriordan
Age 16
St. Paul, IN**

I was amazed by this artwork from the first moment I saw it! The zodiac animals look so real. (Alexander, do you visit the zoo often?) Hiro is my favorite here—he looks so cute and yet so proud at the same time. But Tohru also looks very darling: happy to be with the ones she loves. And as for how to improve, just keep practicing!

Lauralirio Rodriguez
Age 23
Seaside, CA

The detail on this artwork can be explained with no other word but "stunning." Look at all the little details; the little band-aid on Tohru's knee, the plants at their feet, the exquisite pattern on Tohru's dress or the dead little fishy being swatted at by the kitty underneath. It looks like a wonderful place to be a young Kyo, Tohru and Yuki!

Elizabeth Dobak
Age 12
Manassas, VA

Well Elizabeth, your dream has come true! Why did you take three long years to send this awesome work of art to us? The detail on the clothes is absolutely amazing! Kisa-chan looks so very cute in her sad state of cake-less-ness, and the yummy looking cake is making me hungry. Please continue to draw! I want to see more of your talent published in the future!

Linh Truang
Age 13
Rochester, NY

Of all the talented artwork Ling submitted (four in total!) this one was my favorite. Kisa-chan looks so cute in her loli outfit holding a very cuddly-looking tiger. The details are great—I love the shading and her cute little socks. She looks so happy and excited, like she is seeing something wonderful just beyond the page! What are you so happy about Kisa-chan? Please let us know soon!

Jenna Barnes
Age 13
Spencer, IA

Jesse Barnes
Age 13
Spencer, IA

Check out these pictures from twins Jenna and Jesse! Yuki must be very hungry in this picture! Is that drool I see? I guess you can say that his cute little chibi eyes are in fact bigger than his stomach! Will he be able to eat the entire rice ball? Only time will tell. These are some of the cutest chibis I've ever seen.

Danah Macaraig
Age 17
Pomona, NY

Wouldn't it be so nice to take a stroll underneath the cherry blossoms on a breezy spring day? Tohru looks so peaceful here, with her cute hair ties blowing in the breeze. She is holding a daffodil's petal—perhaps to ask if the one she loves, loves her back. "He loves me, he loves me not..."

Angele Salanga
Age 17
Na'alehu, Hawaii

Hana, Tohru and Uo look so sophisticated and beautifu in these original pieces by Angele. I love especially the details in Hana's skirt and Tohru's neckpiece. Tohru's face is also very sweet as well, and I enjoy th fact that this is not the quintessential Furuba style.

Andrea Parra
Age 17
Beaufort, SC

Everyone looks so happy in this picture it is hard not to become happy as well! It looks as even the stoic Kyo is trying hard to resist a cheerful smile. I love the position of the kitty Kyo, and the shading on the colored version is really great! I am sorry you cannot see it here!

Katie Lin Bishop
Age 19
Payson, UT

Hatsuharu looks quite cool in this artwork—letting the dark Hatsu seep through, am I right? His shrugging expression really brings the attitude he is known for to the surface. But how will Rin react to his new fashion choices?

Samantha Giles
Age 13
Duarte, CA

Kyo looks so dashing in this picture with this mysterious mask on! Tohru doesn't seem to mind either, and she looks quite happy at his teasing. But will this "Phantom of Furuba" get the girl in the end of the story? You will have to keep reading to find out!

Jennifer Sawyer
Age 19
Bakersfield, CA

Aww! I want a free kitty! Kisa-chan looks so cute in that cardboard box with all those fuzzy balls of joy. Great job on her little legs and tail—it makes her look all the cuter! They are all so precious, but if I had to choose, I'd have to pick the kitty with the sign. I have wanted to take Kisa-chan home since the first day I saw her!

Thank you so much for all the fan art you have sent in! We have received thousands of wonderful pieces over the years. But from now on, please upload them to the TOKYOPOP website. Go to http://www.tokyopop.com/fansbasket for more info!

TOKYOPOP MANGA SUPPLEMENT

TSUBASA
THOSE WITH WINGS

FROM THE CREATOR OF
FRUITS BASKET!

All ex-thief Kotobuki and her ex-military commander boyfriend Raimon want is a quiet, peaceful life together. But if those seeking a legendary wish-granting wing have anything to say about it, they won't be in retirement for long!

Available wherever books are sold!

FANTASY | OT OLDER TEEN AGE 16+

TSUBASA WO MOTSU MONO © 1995 Natsuki Takaya / HAKUSENSHA

FOR MORE INFORMATION VISIT: WWW.TOKYOPOP.COM

Phantom Dream
volume 1

new manga from Fruits Basket creator Natsuki Takaya!

Tamaki Otoya, the last in an ancient line of summoners, is asked to battle evil forces that threaten mankind. But when this fight turns against the love of his life, will he choose his passion or his destiny?

ON SALE NOW!

Read *Phantom Dream* online at TOKYOPOP.com/PhantomDream

Organize your life with the ultimate
Fruits Basket™
Planner!
By Natsuki Takaya
• Undated pages for maximum flexibility
• Black-and-white art and an 8-page color gallery of your favorite Furuba characters
• Daily, week-at-a-glance, month-at-a-glance sections
Fruits Basket™
Planner
TOKYOPOP
Basket
Planner™
Tuesday
Wednesday
4:00
5:00
6:00
7:00
8:00
9:00
10:00
11:00
Fruits Basket
Planner™
Monday
Tuesday
Read Fruits Basket at www.TOKYOPOP.com/Fruits_Basket
© 1998 Natsuki Takaya / HAKUSENSHA, Inc.

TOKYOPOP MANGA SUPPLEMENT

Fruits Basket
sticker collection
stickers, pinups, and temporary tattoos!!

BEAUTIFY YOUR SURROUNDINGS —AND YOURSELF!— WITH GORGEOUS ART FROM *FRUITS BASKET*!

Pinup Sample Page

Pinup Sample Page

Temp. Tattoo Sample Page

Winner of the American Anime Award for Best Manga

This limited edition art book includes:
- Pinup art of all your favorite *Fruits Basket* characters
- Stickers
- Temporary Tattoos

© 1998 Natsuki Takaya / HAKUSENSHA, Inc

FOR MORE INFORMATION VISIT: WWW.TOKYOPOP.COM

TOKYOPOP MANGA SUPPLEMENT

From the creative minds that brought you the first Princess Ai trilogy

Princess Ai: The Prism of Midnight Dawn

Also Available: Limited time only! Special Edition with bonus Princess Ai DVD

The long-awaited *Princess Ai* sequel has arrived

Volume 1 in Stores Now!

Explore the Princess Ai world at www.TOKYOPOP.com/PrincessAi

TOKYOPOP MANGA SUPPLEMENT

LOVELESS

Volume 8

by Yun Kouga

HOW DO YOU FIND HAPPINESS WHEN YOUR NAME IS LOVELESS?

Ritsuka will have to decide once and for all what his true feelings are about his mysterious (and malevolent) older brother, not to mention where his loyalties lie!

FANTASY | OT OLDER TEEN AGE 16+

© Yun Kouga

ART NOT FINAL

Rated "Must Have" —IGN.com

ON SALE NOW!

Read *LOVELESS* at www.TOKYOPOP.com/onlinemanga

FOR MORE INFORMATION VISIT: WWW.TOKYOPOP.COM

Explore Aqua and Neo-Venezia in a new way!

The anime adaptation of Kozue Amano's ARIA manga is **Now Available on DVD!**

All 13 episodes of the first season in one DVD collection!

NOZOMI ENTERTAINMENT

aria.rightstuf.com

RightStuf!

ARIA
The ANIMATION

DETROIT PUBLIC LIBRARY

3 5674 05049237 1

STOP!

This is the back of the book.
You wouldn't want to spoil a great ending!

This book is printed "manga-style" in the authentic Japanese right-to-left format. Since none of the artwork has been flipped or altered, readers get to experience the story just as the creator intended. You've been asking for it, so TOKYOPOP® delivered: authentic, hot-off-the-press, and far more fun!

DETROIT PUBLIC LIBRARY
TEEN CENTER
5201 WOODWARD AVE.
DETROIT, MI 48202
(313) 833-1000

DIRECTIONS

If this is your first time reading manga-style, here's a quick guide to help you understand how it works.

It's easy... just start in the top right panel and follow the numbers. Have fun, and look for more 100% authentic manga from TOKYOPOP®!

THE MANGA REVOLUTION · LEADING
漫画革命